21 DIRTY TRICKS AT WORK

HOW TO WIN AT OFFICE

POLITICS

COLIN GAUTREY AND MIKE PHIPPS

First published 2005 by Capstone Publishing Limited (a Wiley Company), The Atrium, Southern Gate, Chichester West Sussex, PO19 8SQ

Reprinted January 2007, May 2008

www.wileyeurope.com
Email (for orders and customer service enquiries): cs-books@wiley.co.uk

CIP catalogue records for this book are available from the British Library and the US Library of Congress.

ISBN13: 978-1-841-12657-9 (PB)

Typeset in Meta Normal by Sparks (www.sparks.co.uk).

Substantial discounts on bulk quantities of Capstone books are available to corporations, professional associations and other organizations.

For details telephone John Wiley & Sons on (+44) 1243-770441, fax (+44) 1243770571 or email corporatedevelopment@wiley.co.uk

FSC
Mixed Sources
Product group from well-managed
forests and other controlled sources

Cert no. SGS-COC-2953
www.fsc.org
© 1996 Forest Stewardship Council

CONTENTS

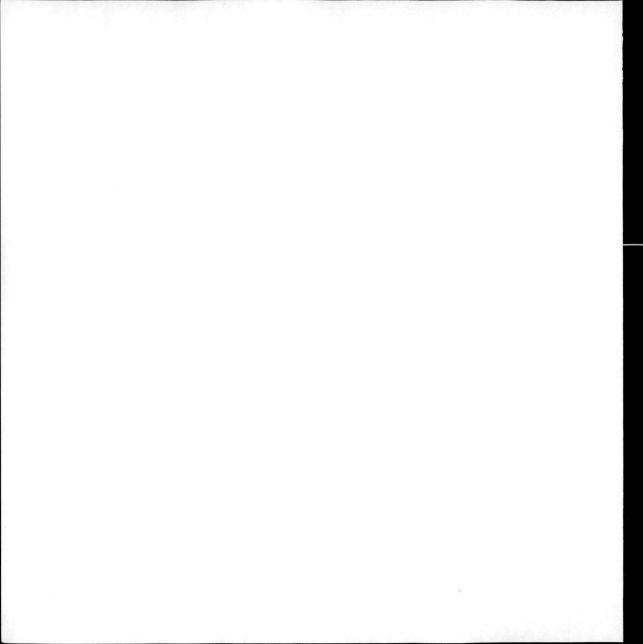

ACKNOWLEDGEMENTS

Whilst two names appear on the cover of this book, behind the scenes lots of great people made direct, indirect and even inadvertent contributions to our writing and thinking. In this small space we would like to acknowledge all those who helped us on our way and who continue to support and inspire us.

- Diane Bartley and Jackie Gautrey, our supportive partners.
- Edward, Oliver, Sarah, Luci and James, our inspirational children.
- Bridget Farrands, Grahame Pitts, Eric Parsloe, Keith Francis and Carmel McConnell for your inspirational mentoring.
- John Moseley our most helpful editor and the team at Capstone Wiley.
- Tim Stockil, Linda Griffiths and all at Arts & Business who helped us.
- Mark Trezona and Martin Duffy at BridgeBuilders for opening the door.
- Claire Davies for her continued support and challenge.
- Wendi Pasco and Penny Albertella at Laurel Consulting for all your support.
- Julie Hay for opening up transactional analysis (TA) and neuro-linguistic programming (NLP).
- Annie Gray, Naomi Biggs and David Wilson for taking a risk on us when we were young.
- All our business partners and everyone in the Politics at Work Associate Network for helping us to take these ideas into organizations.
- All the delegates and clients we have worked with who told us their stories, added to our understanding and challenged our thinking.
- Everyone who motivated us by saying we were mad to call our company Politics at Work!
- Machiavelli, without whom this book would probably not have been possible!

INTRODUCTION: IMMUNITY OR IGNORANCE?

This is a book about lies. It is an unpleasant collection of some of the most common Dirty Tricks and political games that get played in organizations. We know that there will be controversy and concern about this material. One of our fiercest critics has already dismissed our work as 'just helping people to lie more effectively', and we are aware that by encouraging you to read and learn from these examples, that we are handing you a moral dilemma. There is a positive intention behind our work however. We are going to expose Machiavellian managers, get them on the run and leave them no place to hide.

This is also a book about hope and integrity. We know that the vast majority of people in organizations want to do good work, to be of service and to benefit in turn. But they are frequently frustrated or sabotaged by unhelpful politics and abuses of power. Our mission is to do something positive about that. Not only do we share these Dirty Tricks with you, we also provide expert advice on what to do when they stop you doing what is right for the organization. This help is based on our extensive work with senior managers from a diverse range of organizations large and small. If you are determined to act with integrity, you might like to think of this book as career antivirus software.

These Dirty Tricks are shared with you on the understanding that to know them, means you will be forewarned and therefore forearmed should you come across Machiavellian management in your organization, which you will. We do NOT expect you to try them out on 'Jerry' at the next project meeting. If you do, then you had better hope that Jerry has not read this book.

We believe that the more people who know how to recognize these games and have learned our useful strategies for tackling them, the less likely Machiavellian managers are to use them. Rather like the Nigerian Email Scam[1], which was initially quite successful on the Internet. The more people who heard about it, discussed it and passed their knowledge on, the fewer people got caught out by it. The exposure of Dirty Tricks, dragging them from the shadows into the light, is to reduce their power. This is our higher purpose.

We propose that ignorance, ambivalence and reticence are no longer viable options. Holding up your hands and declaring that you 'don't do politics' is no longer good enough. Machiavellian management have been exploiting this outlook for too long. In this book we propose that developing inoculation, immunity and effective antidotes against negative politics will be more productive, for all.

By their very nature, we acknowledge that all organizations are political and that it is a competitive world out there. We are not naïve enough to believe that a Utopian organization exists, or is even that desirable. However, the downside to these Dirty Tricks and political games is firstly that the financial cost of internal power struggles and politicking can now measured in billions[2]. The second is that focus, energy and commitment drain from the organization, whilst more focused competitors laugh all the way to the bank. Thirdly, the talented, bright, articulate, future leaders of the organization (who we have aggressively head-hunted, selected and groomed) become disenchanted, burned

---

[1] The Nigerian Email Scam is a spam e-mail that still circulates around the web today. In it someone claims to be connected to a wealthy but allegedly oppressed Nigerian diplomat or businessperson and asks that you help them to get their rightful wealth out of the country, which the government are blocking. They offer to share the fortune with you by placing the money directly into your bank account and then when they arrive in the UK, you agree to pay it back minus the massive commission they are offering you. All you need do is to send them your bank sort code and account number and – here is the con – £500 for administration costs, and they will wire the fortune directly across.

[2] The Reed Report from 2002 estimated the cost at £7.8bn for the UK based just on the time spent dealing with issues around power and politics. It did not factor in the cost of lost customers, cancelled contracts, damage to reputation, the loss of morale and the talent drain.

out, beaten up, cynical ... and then they leave. Ask yourself, how high is the talent body count in your organization? Learning to more appropriately manage the political dynamics in the organization delivers benefits not only to the emotional balance sheet, but to the financial balance sheet too!

These political Dirty Tricks are more than just a career-threatening nuisance; they also form part of the political backdrop to all the great recent organizational scandals. Enron, WorldCom, Equitable Life, Shell (oil reserves) and even the English Football Association (Sven-Goran Eriksson and Mark Pallios) were mired in power struggles and negative politics. The more that you scratch the surface of these scandals, the more unhelpful politicking you find. Why do these games seem to flourish and thrive in our organizations? Why do our competency frameworks, role specifications, vision and values fail to protect us from this type of exploitation? Why is there such a gap between the rhetoric and the reality?

1 Magnetic north vs true north

The work of leadership is to articulate the vision and values of the organization and set the strategic direction. Stephen Covey likens this work to setting the compass on behalf of the followers. But increasingly followers are getting an acute sense of where their own internal compass is leading them and are ever more determined to act upon it. When the two versions of north do not align, in the gap, there is a fertile breeding ground for the politics of self-interest to prevail, especially if the organizational culture somehow inhibits open conversations. For many, just casually raising the possibility that they might be looking to further their career elsewhere is a 'career decision'.

2 The rate of change

The rate of organizational change continues to accelerate, and this is a significant factor in encouraging unhelpful political behaviour. More than ever, followers are asking; why bother being dedicated to following a long-term vision and being true to the values when no one is guaranteed to be here next week? Why invest in relationships, when results are everything? Given that negative political games can be effective in the shorter term, and given that everyone is overworked and stressed, it is hardly surprising that more people are seduced into short-term thinking. Even our organizational language can betray our lack of faith in the long-term strategy. People talk more and more about 'quick wins' and 'low hanging fruit' and are frequently rewarded and congratulated when they do so. But what is the longer term, hidden cost of this short-termism?

3 The flatter structure

There was a time when our organizations had clear hierarchical structures. We all knew where the buck stopped and who the powerful people were because they had job titles (and other overt, hedonistic trappings), which made it clear to everyone involved. Of course this state of affairs still encouraged game playing as people competed to get an ever-tighter grip on the greasy pole. But then came the new age of flatter structures, matrix management and non-hierarchical organizations, designed to encourage team working, co-operation and greater productivity.

Unfortunately the new reality for most organizations is that political game playing has increased[3]. Regardless of job titles, everyone knows who the powerful people are, and navigate accordingly. It seems that in the power vacuum, created by removing status and authority as the major orientation points for power, these gamey ways of transacting power continued along as if nothing had happened, and in many cases, just got more sophisticated and damaging!

4 Lonely at the top?

And as if the challenge was not difficult enough already, for directors and leaders there is the additional burden generated by the sense of isolation that many senior people talk about in their more honest, yet vulnerable moments. This was confirmed by research conducted by Leaders in London[4] in June 2004, which found that 31% of senior managers considered loneliness to be the worst part of their job. The same research revealed

---

[3] Linda Holbeche in *Politics in Organisations 2004* found that '69% of respondents in the 2002 survey reported that political behaviour was rife – and on the increase'.

[4] Leaders in London 2004 was an International Leadership Summit held in London, which included speakers such as Jack Welch, Michael Porter and Robert Kaplan. See www.leadersinlondon.com

that 'office politics' topped the most hated list at 46%. More and more they ask external consultants and coaches about 'what is really going on' in their organization. And the followers, who have an acute enough antennae to detect this isolation, and those who have already signed up to the politics of self-interest, take this as tacit permission to exploit the situation.

5 The absence of language and understanding

We notice that words like power and politics have strongly negative connotations for most people. Because of this strong reaction, these are topics which many are uncomfortable to raise let alone confront. In the first place, the absence of real understanding about power and politics and the lack of a suitable language framework, has led to these vital and productive conversations being easily missed, closed down, declared inappropriate, misunderstood or ignored. The challenge for leadership is to get the conversations about power and politics on the table, and to do it constructively. The ostrich mentality usually exacerbates the problem as silence (or ignorance) on the subject will be interpreted by Machiavellian types as an opportunity.

Secondly, making these issues taboo fuels the mystery and mystique, meaning that even some of the most senior people we get to work with are ignorant of all but the most obvious and clumsy political strategies. Finally, and most serious of all, is the way in which even our most skilled and talented clients are seemingly unable to find strategies to deal with these difficult situations effectively, without either 'playing the game' or resorting to fighting fire with fire, with predictable and frequently dire consequences.

6 The problem of management literature

Take a look on the bookshelves at Waterstones or visit the Amazon website and you discover a huge number of books all about power and politics. Normally this would be an encouraging sign, but a closer look reveals that the vast majority are all about 'playing the game', getting one over on your colleagues and justifying the politics of self-interest. Too many authors have spent time educating us to play WIN/LOSE strategies. Recent best-sellers highlight the problem; *The 48 Laws of Power* (mostly about how 'wise' Machiavelli was, with no regard to the damage these strategies promote); *The Way of the Rat* (apparently the only way to get ahead is to be a bigger rat than everyone else); *100+ Tactics for Office Politics* (which are mostly strategies of self-interest, and damn the organization).

This book is different and will break the mould by proposing more productive strategies and ways forward. We notice that most books about office politics concentrate on personality types, alleging that type X people do this, or that type Y do it a different way. Whilst these generalizations are helpful, more needs to be done to explain the specific strategies and Dirty Tricks involved. This is vital because Dirty Tricks appear to cut across personality types, all types are susceptible to the temptation to act in negatively political ways, so to warn against only certain types of people is to ignore significant threats from elsewhere. This is why we are concentrating primarily on the tricks, tactics, strategies and games that people use, regardless of type.

7 The problem with culture and unwritten rules

If we search out and recruit and nurture the top talents in our industry, should we not be doing more to ensure that they direct their time, energy and talent into doing good work instead of 'playing the game'? People take their cue about 'how things get done around here' not from the declared vision and values, but from the unwritten rules and codes of conduct from their seniors. So the challenge is the extent to which our senior managers are setting the correct example, or are they unwittingly cloning the next generation of Machiavellian executives? Is the competition in your marketplace not fierce enough already without handing your competitors another advantage by being caught up in your own political infighting?

8 The challenge of childhood

Before we even arrive in the world of work, we have already learned at a very young age a whole set of coping mechanisms and less than helpful political behaviour programmes as children. Many of these Dirty Tricks have their psychological roots in childhood, where our first experiments in manipulation and the testing of our personal power take place.

Anyone with small children will know how they will test out various indirect manipulation strategies on their parents and pay close attention to which work and which don't. In addition, further development of these skills continues in the playground and in the classroom where tactics are practised and refined.

By the time we arrive in the world of work we have already had a great deal of experience with power and politics and have, at a deep level, engrained a set of mental programmes and assumptions about how these dynamics work. If you are not convinced that every director has an internalized seven-year-old child in control of their behaviour from time to time, you should spend more time observing the board when they meet. Have you ever noticed how apparently professional exchanges suddenly tip over into 'my dad's bigger than your dad' or 'it's my ball and I'm taking it home'? In addition to learning positive political skills we also need to do some unlearning or reprogramming of some of these deeply engrained thinking patterns.

9 These political games work!

The most depressing news is that these games get played because they work, at least in the short-term and those who play them are sometimes rightly confident that circumstances might change before they get detected. But now the time for change has come. By writing a book exposing these Dirty Tricks we will soon start to make inroads into removing the potency of their players.

WHAT IS A DIRTY TRICK?
For a series of moves to qualify as a Dirty Trick for our collection, all of the following conditions exist:

- A lack of trust that behaving authentically will be effective.
- At least one player needs to believe that they have the right to exploit others, or to be one up at someone else's expense.
- Something is at stake, or there is an opportunity to exploit.
- A need to cover something up, restrict or distort the real situation or information.

- Frequently, a surface communication of helpfulness masquerading as a cover-up position for unhelpfulness.
- A strong desire to act out of self-interest rather than serving the organization.
- A negative pay-off for the victim, and an apparent victory for the protagonist

If at first you don't see some of them, look again; they're usually there, just beneath the surface. Note that they are more than just ways of behaving, they are all tactical in their intent and involve a motive, a lie, and a one up/one down pay-off. Scratch the surface of any of these Dirty Tricks, and you will find a lie.

TRANSACTIONAL ANALYSIS
Throughout the book you will notice that we have sometimes referred to the person who makes the opening moves in a Dirty Trick, and who is working with ulterior intent, as the 'persecutor'. Also that we refer to the person on the receiving end as the 'victim', and two other roles, 'rescuer' and 'bystander'.

These labels are based on the work of Steve Karpman and others from the field of transactional analysis. Despite our work being rooted in social psychology, this is not an academic or psychological text. For those interested in developing deeper understanding in this arena, we have recommended several books in the bibliography at the end of this book.

HOW TO GET THE MOST FROM THIS BOOK
To bring the Dirty Tricks to life we have written a story in seven chapters that follows a few key players in the Xennic Corporation through the political mire. We use this to illustrate in a true-to-life setting how these Dirty Tricks are played out in organizational life. Each chapter of the story is followed by a trio of tricks, each of which describes how the trick works, links back to the story and then provides advice on how to handle it.

Our suggestion is that you read each chapter in turn, consider how this relates to your work environment and then try to identify the tricks before you turn the page where all is revealed. In this way as you progress through the book you will be developing your own political intelligence with our help. We suspect that you will skip around but please remember that our purpose is to help you to develop your skills and help you to survive in the world of work without endangering your integrity, so think carefully about the issues presented.

You will notice that with each of the Dirty Tricks we have assessed the level of threat and potential damage at stake. These ratings have been developed as a guide so that you can be alerted to the more damaging tactics that Machiavelli is fond of. The statistics are based on our experience with helping managers navigate these situations and may not necessarily be how you might view them, especially if you are currently caught up in some of this unhelpful politicking.

We have also provided a series of power tips throughout the book. These are designed to highlight and focus you on some of the best practice ideas contained in our work. There is not always a direct correlation between the Dirty Trick and the power tip, but from time to time you will notice a delightful and helpful synergy. Taking heed of these will help you to develop your own personal power.

HEALTH WARNING

It is impossible for us to know as much as you do about any difficult situation you find yourself in at work. Because of that you need to read what we've got to say about each trick and very carefully tailor it to your personal circumstances and skills. We cannot accept responsibility for your actions (only you can do this); however, we are confident that you will fare better if you carefully adapt our insights.

TIME FOR CHANGE

The great organizational performance improvement opportunity of the 21st century is not going to be focused on TQM, ISO, IIP, Six Sigma or any of these other process type initiatives, great though they are. The real opportunity is to get each of us learning about how we can use our personal power to cut through unhelpful self-interest more effectively, creating instead a climate and culture of positive power and politics. As a business we focus on helping organizations and individuals to tap into the wasted resources and motivation so that they can influence with integrity. This book is based on this experience and has some pretty neat ideas about how you can get started with this work.

Imagine what you could do if you no longer had to 'play politics' at work to get things done? How much time would you save? How much more effective could you, your team and your organization become? How much more rewarding would work become? It is time to transform the political culture of our organizations and renegotiate the political contract. The challenge has begun and we are pleased that you have joined us. Now, together, let's get Machiavelli on the run.

CHAPTER ONE

DESTINY
BECKONS

In foul temper, Ben pushed his way through the revolving doors of Xennic corporate HQ. He hated revolving doors, mostly because you couldn't slam them shut behind you. Not that he was an 'angry young exec' but that the Xennic building was already starting to become the embodiment for all that was wrong with his shining career. Revolving doors are of course both impractical and metaphoric.

Ben was annoyed with himself for saying 'yes' when he wanted to say 'no'. But what else could he have done? Jerry, his boss had strongly suggested to all, that to say 'no' to the weekend strategy workshop would be a 'career decision'. Spending five working days per week with these characters was abhorrent enough, yet to cap it all, this was to have been the weekend when he had planned a special trip for the family! Strategic away days were important, but anyone wanting to discuss 'work–life balance' with Ben would find it a short topic of conversation today. In conversations around the water cooler Ben's colleagues had been quick to dub the strategic away day using the acronym SAD, which is both depressing and rather apt perhaps.

The rent-a-guard on the front desk barely acknowledged his presence, fixated as he was on watching something on a screen. Ben swiped his card through the slot allowing the turnstile to rotate him slowly into another day at the office. What fun awaited he wondered as he made his way to the lifts.

Alone in the lift, he quickly 'adjusted himself' only then remembering the new security cameras that had been installed. Ah well, another cheap thrill for the security guy. The cameras had been fitted 'for your safety and security' the small notice said. Ben had taken it as another sign of the organizations' big brother culture creeping over them.

He wondered how and when he had got so paranoid and cynical. Originally he had been delighted to be headhunted for this job from a significant competitor where he had been working. Along with the increased salary and status he was especially pleased as he thought it meant that he could leave the power struggles, bickering and office politicking behind him. Ben now realized that this made him naïve as well as cynical, as at times this place seemed as bad, if not worse.

Not that he wasn't good at his job, he was, it was just that at times it seemed that unseen forces in the organization were conspiring in the shadows against him. He had genuinely wanted to do well, to make a contribution and to exploit his talents for the benefit of all, but as one colleague had confided to him recently in an unguarded moment, 'being good is never going to be good enough, Ben'.

When Ben asked her what she meant she explained that the 'great game' was all about whom and what you knew. Critical was how you looked and sounded, rather that what you said. Style was now more important than substance and that anything other than toeing the party line would lead to 'career shortening activity' as the organizational immune system kicked in to expel the 'virus'. Above all the ability to influence people and events was now the key skill required. Ben had originally dismissed these views as those of the bitter and twisted minority, but these days he was increasingly beginning to wonder.

Political correctness might be the order of the day, 'respect and togetherness' might be on the Corporate Values Statement, but other attitudes always lurked in the shadows, and these days the shadows seemed to be getting longer and darker.

Certainly anyone who had faith in the 360 degree appraisal process as a measure of who got promoted and how you got rewarded were deluding themselves. Everyone knew that the reality was that performance evaluations were rigged to fit the distribution curve, and that the politicking and negotiating around the process was more important than what you delivered.

Ben emerged from the lift – yes, they really were that slow in this building – and walked across the open-plan office to his desk. The floor was deserted except for Jerry in his goldfish bowl corner office, yelling down the phone at some poor unfortunate who had presumably dared to have an opinion of their own, and even more stupidly, had decided to share it with this mini despot at 07.30 on a Monday morning.

Ben plugged in his laptop and punched the play button on his voice mail. 'You have … 17 new messages,' the metallic voice chirped, Ben's heart sank. Mostly they were just small stuff, chaff that clogged up your day and got in the way, but one got his attention, a message from Spencer in Finance asking him why he had not attended the Project Genesis meeting last Friday. What the hell was Project Genesis? Sometimes he wondered if he knew what was going on, or if he was losing his grip. He was certainly out of the loop on this one.

Ben realized he should never have given up smoking. As a smoker you get to go to this hovel of a room in the basement to partake and inhale at regular intervals. The added bonus is that you get to mingle with the disparate band of other tobacco dependent individuals, many of whom were also senior managers and directors. In between lungfuls of stinking blue smoke, trivia and gossip, astonishing indiscretions were often made, and you really got to know what was going on. Had Ben realized that giving up smoking would lead to such political isolation he would never have stopped. Okay, so he might have died sooner, but at least he would know what Project Genesis was.

He checked his other messages, rooted back though his online diary and inbox messages for any trace of Project Genesis. Nothing. Not on the company intranet, but no surprise there! Very strange. Perhaps Spencer was mistaken; perhaps it was a wind up? Ben decided that he had better discuss it with Jerry in their Monday morning 'catch-up' at 09.30. Quite why he needed to 'catch-up' with Jerry given that he had just spent the whole damn weekend with the ogre was beyond him, but at least Jerry would probably know about Project Genesis, being a 40-Marlboro-a-day man.

Jerry finally hollered for Ben at 11:10, close to two hours behind schedule. Ben had been sitting nearby during this time watching a stream of visitors being ushered into

Jerry's office, and his time slot. Many were clutching large files but he also noted that they all carried the same 'rabbit in the headlights' look in their faces. Ben entered Jerry's office with some trepidation. 'Ben, sit down,' barked Jerry without even looking up from his papers. Could it be possible that Jerry had somehow risen to such heights without ever hearing about interpersonal skills, politeness, friendliness, respect, etc? Ben smiled inwardly, shifted uncomfortably and noted the extent of his optimistic stupidity.

Before Ben had a chance to draw breath, Jerry launched right in. 'Ben, I've got a development opportunity for you.' Ben was caught by surprise since he'd been steeling himself for some bad news. Perhaps he was getting too cynical in his old age. Maybe this was going to be the golden opportunity he needed to get into the 'in crowd'. 'I'm all ears Jerry' Ben said in an unexpectedly cheery tone.

Jerry continued, 'We want you to take control of Project Genesis'. Ben reeled and held on to the sides of his chair, he hoped Jerry wouldn't notice. Jerry blathered on... 'As you know it is a business critical initiative which is a year late and we're nearly £12m in the hole, so we need someone to take over from Mark who has been leading it. Everyone believes that Mark has been doing a great job in difficult circumstances, the MD even said so at the last shareholders' meeting, so the main task now is to sail the ship safely into port.'

Ben was stunned, too stunned to reply for a moment. Project Genesis was 'business critical' and he hadn't even heard of it. Either it's a well-kept secret or he really was out of the loop these days, and given that this organization was pathologically incapable of keeping anything secret ... Ben's discomfort increased. During this mental sojourn he missed Jerry mentioning that the chairman had recently, very publicly, reconfirmed his support of Mark as project leader in difficult times, but despite this, for reasons not yet disclosed, a change of leadership was now thought necessary.

Ben focused back in on Jerry who was sledgehammering on. '...and you don't need me to tell you that the board have high hopes from Project Genesis and it is going to be a significant milestone on anyone's CV and career at Xennic. From today I want you to clear the decks, drop everything else and get over to the Luton office where you'll be based from the start of next week. Now, I'm running late for the board meeting, so no time to catch up on anything else now but I will check in with you later. Congratulations Ben, oh, and don't let me down.'

And with that, the whirlwind that is Jerry swept out of the office clutching a Marlboro. Ben half expected the huge plate glass window to implode in the vacuum. Ben was still sitting in stunned silence five minutes later when Jerry's personal assistant came in to see if he was okay.

Eventually he found himself back at his desk discussing Project Genesis over the partition with Lewis, a colleague with unbelievably bad hair. Lewis laughed and told Ben that Project Genesis was not some great corporate secret but was in fact Project Achilles. It had been renamed last week as part of a rationalization of initiatives, although the cynical Lewis really believed it was just to make it sound better and to stem the flow of people angling to get off it.

Ben knew that Project Achilles was indeed a big deal and he suddenly felt a bit better about the whole affair; well maybe not the part about going to Luton. How the hell was he going to convince Hanna – his wife – that Luton was a good move for the family? Yes, this might indeed be a great opportunity. Certainly Mark, who had been leading it had done very well out of it, because Lewis had heard that he was now off to Florida, to head up Project Horizons. Perhaps Luton would not be so bad in the short term if Florida became the next stop for him too.

Ben commented that it was good that Mark's hard work on Achilles had been recognized by the organization. Lewis looked at Ben with the sort of patronizing sympathy that politicians usually reserve for their constituents. '... And you don't think that Mark, being the MD's son-in-law, has anything to do with his Florida appointment?' The brief moment of happiness that Ben had experienced evaporated.

CHAPTER ONE: MENTORING INTERVENTION

Whilst this first chapter is fictional it nevertheless portrays a scenario similar to one that is played in organizations of all types, all around the world. A bright, talented young thing, new into the job and full of high hopes, finds that their best efforts and positive intentions are gradually strangled by unhelpful establishment politics.

As we stated in the introduction, our main purpose is to equip people with critical career-enhancing knowledge about the complexities of organizations. We do not seek to encourage Dirty Tricks, far from it. Rather we aim to expose them for what they often are: self-serving tactics used by manipulative yet savvy people to get their own way, always at the expense of another, and often at the expense of the whole organization.

Before we analyze this first episode and we introduce you to the first three Dirty Tricks, treat yourself to a brief time out for some one-to-one political coaching. To get the most out of this exercise, view it as a real development opportunity. Ask yourself the following questions to check the levels of your own political savvy, astuteness, innocence or ignorance.

- What should Ben have done differently in his meeting with Jerry?
- Why do you believe that Project Genesis was re-named?
- What warning signs are there about Project Genesis/Achilles?
- Should Ben take up smoking again?
- What could it cost Ben if he takes up this 'opportunity'?
- How might the organization suffer if Jerry continues in power?
- What has really been going on behind the scenes?
- Luton and Florida both have international airports, so does that make both places okay?

The critical question to ask yourself is: if you were in Ben's position, what would you do next? The following pages will help to shed light on your answer as we explore the Dirty Tricks in play. The more politically savvy amongst you will have detected three tricks at work here. For each trick that you identified either breathe a sign of relief or hang your head in shame.

THE DIRTY TRICKS IN CHAPTER ONE

DIRTY TRICK NO. 1: FALL GUY/THE PATSY
Assigning projects or tasks that are destined to fail to an expendable manager so that they can be blamed for the failure, and/or to reassign favoured employees away from reputation-threatening failure.

DIRTY TRICK NO. 2: DEVELOPMENT OPPORTUNITY
The tactic of motivating someone to take on a task, project or assignment they might reasonably refuse, by pretending it is a development opportunity.

DIRTY TRICK NO. 3: KISS LIKE JUDAS
Declaring public support for an embattled project or individual, whilst privately plotting for change behind the scenes: 'I am more convinced than ever that Mark is the right person to lead the team through these difficult days.'

DIRTY TRICK NO. 1

THE FALL GUY/THE PATSY[1]

Assigning projects or tasks that are destined to fail to an expendable manager so that they can be blamed for the failure, and/or to reassign favoured employees away from reputation-threatening failure.

---

[1] A person who is ridiculed, victimized or deceived and it has been suggested to us that this label originates from Chicago gangsters from the American prohibition period.

Projects in organizations fail all the time; it's a fact. Sometimes they fail due to incompetence, lack of resources, internal politicking, competitor activity or other mitigating circumstances. But how the organization reacts and manages this difficult situation is critical and tells us a lot about the true corporate values.

The more politically astute will have detected this game at the heart of our story. Poor Ben is apparently being set up as the *Fall Guy* without realizing it, by being assigned Project Genesis (ironically his Achilles), which sounds very much as if it is more likely to fail than succeed. Furthermore Mark, son-in-law of the MD, would appear to be doing a great job running the project into the ground, and is now being rescued from imminent career-threatening failure by his superiors and transferred onto a more 'career enhancing' project. Florida or Luton? It's a tough choice!

When projects are about to fail, many of those involved will use all sorts of political tactics and games to extricate themselves from the situation. Perhaps Mark has been pulling some political strings? The most common tactic is getting powerful allies and stakeholders to manoeuvre for reassignment on their behalf. This could involve their line managers or friendly directors; in this case family in high places! When reassigned they can then appear less like the 'rats deserting the sinking ship' and are able to take up a position which provides an opportunity to express apparently sincere regret at not being around to assist and see things through. When Mark has to brief the Achilles Team on his departure from the project, no doubt his speech will peppered with such typical 'regrets at moving on at such an exciting time for the project' and 'profound disappointment at not being around for the climax, but sometimes sacrifices have to be made'.

As each person deserts an apparently doomed project, be it leader or team member, their places are frequently taken by *Fall Guys* and *Patsies*, many of whom have probably been told by powerful others to look upon their secondment as a 'development opportunity'. More on these opportunities later.

The inevitable consequence of this type of collective, negative political activity is that energy, time, resource and commitment are all diverted away from the project at the critical time of need. This usually exacerbates the situation and sometimes triggers accelerating failure when success still might have been possible. Also, more and more people get involved and hooked into making moves and 'playing the game' instead of getting on and doing project-saving work. That said, regardless of the project or its current status, who in their right mind would really want to move to Luton?

The time consumed by each of the participants in this political drama represents a significant opportunity cost. There is also a corresponding loss on the emotional balance sheet as trust and goodwill are seriously eroded by the Machiavellian antics. Whilst Ben might be politically naïve, he is nevertheless good at his job and well intentioned. Even if he does manage to turn the project around the chances are that he will not trust Jerry or Mark and will feel that the emotional contract with his employers is null and void. He is most likely to move on again, probably to a competitor. He will take his talent, authenticity and inside knowledge with him. Is he likely to have good words to say about working at Xennic? We suspect not.

Specialist students of Dirty Tricks at work will be enthralled at an interesting twist to *Fall Guy*, where a project is deliberately set up with built-in failure. In this version the *Fall Guy* is assigned to it from the start, along with as many *Patsies* as can be collectively dumped at any one time without arising undue suspicion. Again, the tactic is to demote or remove individuals who do not fit with the political ambitions of the key power-brokers.

GAME STATS: THE FALL GUY/PATSY

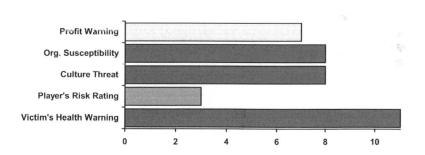

PROFIT WARNING 7/10 (OVERALL, WHAT RISK DOES THIS PRESENT TO THE BOTTOM LINE FOR THE ORGANIZATION?)

Much of the damage has already been done before this trick comes into play. Therefore the real hit on the bottom line is the lack of creative effort to turn the project around, or to exit quickly. The time spent as people re-position themselves can add to the opportunity cost as well.

ORG. SUSCEPTIBILITY 8/10 (HOW PRONE IS AN ORGANIZATION TO THIS TYPE OF BEHAVIOUR?)

When a project starts to fail, the temptation is great, particularly if there is a strong culture of negative politics within the organization and there are very powerful people at the top of the organization who lack integrity.

CULTURE THREAT 8/10 (HOW DOES THIS AFFECT THE ORGANIZATION CULTURE, AND STAFF MORALE?)

This trick more than any other promotes political games amongst all ranks. Therefore playing this trick is very damaging to a healthy culture, which benefits from straight talking and creative effort.

PLAYER'S RISK RATING 3/10 (HOW RISKY IS IT FOR THE PLAYER TO PLAY THIS DIRTY TRICK AND RISK EXPOSURE?)

In reality not a huge risk since the ones playing it are the most powerful people in the organization who, if accused, are likely to be able to tough it out until the shareholders have had enough.

VICTIM'S HEALTH WARNING 7/10 TO 11/10 (WHAT RISK IS THE VICTIM PLACED UNDER WHEN THIS TRICK IS IN PLAY?)

Much depends on where you sit. If you are positioned to head up the project, early diagnosis and treatment is essential. The longer it is left the worse it gets. Frankly the odds are really stacked against you if all the power players are colluding.

THE ANTIDOTE: FALL GUY/THE PATSY

As you will have noticed from the story, being good at your job is not going to be sufficient insurance against this Dirty Trick. Considerable care is needed because of the Victim's Health Warning, the highest score in the book. This is a big ugly one to get landed with, so we will spend more time on helping you to handle this one than any other Dirty Trick.

The advice that follows applies if you are in the top job, or are playing a senior role in the *Fall Guy* project. If you have realized you could be caught up with this trick, the good news is that at least you have some awareness about the situation you are in and the dilemma you face. Many *Fall Guys* stagger blindly on until the inevitable smacks them in the face. The bad news of course is that this is still a very uncomfortable place to be.

Before we start looking at what to do, ask yourself the following 'self coaching' questions to separate out the facts from your fantasies about the situation. This is the first step to political recovery.

- Why do you think this is a *Fall Guy* project?
- What evidence do you have to support this belief?
- When did you get assigned?
- What reasons were you given for your selection?
- Why do you think you were really chosen?
- What makes you think the 'powers that be' consider it to be a *Fall Guy* project?
- What might be the cost to you of getting out?
- What is the simplest thing you could do?
- What is the most radical thing you could do?

The uncomfortable truth is that someone, somewhere has probably lined you up for this fall, and at some stage you took the bait. Now it is likely to be difficult to get out of this situation productively and with your integrity intact.

If as a result of the questions above you are convinced that you have been positioned to take the fall, you have a few choices. Firstly you could brush up your CV and await the inevitable. Secondly you could confront Machiavelli assertively and seek a constructive debate to move the project forward – or kill it quickly. Finally, you can exert all your skills and work hard to make the project a success against all the odds. We believe that if you are well-prepared you should do all three, except the bit about waiting.

Much of the solution to this problem is standard best practice for any project that needs turning around. All of these have their supporters and their opposition. Although this is not a book about general business skills, it is worth quickly restating the basic steps needed when turning around a project. Then we can turn our attention to what to do differently because there is an additional political twist that makes this a *Fall Guy* project.

1 **Identify stakeholders**. Anyone who is anyone to do with the project. These range from directors, to customers and everyone in between. Anyone in fact who will be affected in some way by the project (whether successful or not).
2 **Canvass stakeholder positions**. Select those who have the strongest interest in the project and share your vision for the project. Seek to understand their views towards the project. Generally are they for or against success?
3 **Revisit business case**. Is it still valid and accurate?
4 **Analyze progress**. Even if you have been in position for a while, take a long hard look at what has happened to date. What successes and failures have there been?
5 **Identify key issues**. What are the things getting in the way of progress? What are the showstoppers? For instance, insufficient resources, system failures, technical faults, slow decision making etc.
6 **Stakeholder issues**. Return to the key stakeholders with your analysis of the issues. Seek their views, agreement and support in resolving the issues.
7 **Reset plans**. In the light of everything you have learned, assess the impact on the existing plans and propose alterations.
8 **Communication**. Develop fast and efficient methods for keeping your stakeholders abreast on progress.
9 **Make it happen!**

The real challenge however is navigating through the murky political waters that separate a standard project failure from an intended failure. This is where we leave the standard textbook advice, which often relies on the assumptions that the people you interact with will be honest with you. If you've been set up it will be extremely difficult to get straight and honest answers from Machiavelli, but not impossible.

What are the differences between an ailing project and a *Fall Guy* project? The chief difference is that one or more powerful individuals within the business have invested political capital in the project's failure. They are also likely to have made moves to ensure that the project crashes. Since you've been given the covert task of leading the project through to failure, they are more likely to work against your efforts to turn it around and thereby protect their political investment.

But don't let this put you off. If you are skilled and determined you can still win with integrity, but you will need to take additional steps to protect yourself and maximize your chances.

1 **Your bottom line**. What is the minimum you are prepared to accept as an outcome to this situation (not the project)? For instance, being seen to be assertive in a difficult situation and maintain your integrity.
2 **Assess influence**. For each of your stakeholders, assign a number which represents their ability to influence the project: 10 being very high level of influence, 1 being totally lame.
3 **Assess support**. From all you've seen and heard, if you believe a particular stakeholder is against the project, put a minus sign by their score above.
4 **Business bottom line**. At what point would you pull the plug on the project, even if it puts you at risk? At some stage you may choose to turn up the heat by laying it on the line at a stakeholder meeting. Consider adding a new milestone to the project to table a continuance/kill decision.
5 **Stakeholder benefits**. Once you have sought views on the issues, line up the stakeholders and for each write down a few reasons why they would benefit if the project failed and how they could benefit if the project succeeded. If you can't think of benefits for each stakeholder on both success and failure, get some help from your trusted

supporters. If you can find a way in which the most opposed stakeholder can benefit from the project succeeding you have a seed of hope.

6 **Work the extremes**. Prioritize the stakeholders to work on. Start with the highest scorers, your supporters and then move to those in the murky depths of the scoreboard, the adversaries and opponents.

7 **Supporters**. Meet individually with them. Restate your visions and discuss the benefits they will gain from success. Share your concerns and ask for help, support and advice on how to win for the good of the business. Invest significant time and energy here, which is the best place to create political momentum.

8 **Adversaries**. Drawing on the confidence you have gained from your supporters, now start to meet with those opposed to project success. Again discuss your vision and the benefits you believe they will gain. Seek views and insights into the problems they have with your project and seek to negotiate support. Do not expect too much of them or spend too much time and energy in trying to convert them; remember that they have invested elsewhere.

9 **Remain alert**. You cannot win all the time. So even if all your opponents have come on side, remain vigilant. Watch for other Dirty Tricks and tactics that could be used by Machiavellian types. Stay close to your supporters and get them active on your behalf.

No, it's not easy, but neither is it impossible to make rapid progress on turning around a *Fall Guy* project. But you do need to be careful.

Probably the key opposition that you need to confront, and sooner rather than later, is the person you believe set you up. If you've followed the steps above you should be in a strong position to know how powerful they are in the larger community of stakeholders. Bear this in mind when you decide to confront them. Starting a direct conversation with them may not achieve immediate success but it does have several very important advantages as a starting point.

1 It demonstrates your determination to do the right thing for the business.

2 It flags your self-confidence, assertiveness and political savvy to Machiavellian types.

3 It reduces the need for escalation and attrition, whereby the game spins out of control and more bystanders and rescuers get involved, increasing the complexity of the situation and consuming more resources.

These key advantages are always available to us when we deal directly with Machiavellian types and this advice holds true for every game to be found in this book. Machiavellian types won't often be invited into productive dialogue, but when we are successful with this approach, then everyone usually benefits.

Clearly you have a right to be disappointed, upset or angry at being set up as a 'fall guy'. Use these strong feelings to motivate yourself into taking action, but keep them under control whilst you actually intervene. It may well be that one 'pay-off' for these gamey individuals is to see you upset, angry or both. They may well be looking forward to seeing you 'lose it' so that they can claim the moral high ground, or perhaps pretend shock or surprise at your behaviour. In situations like these you need to engage your emotional intelligence rather than your raw emotions, and act with courage and assertion rather than heroics and aggression. Remember you will probably want to keep your integrity and self-respect intact.

Having prepared yourself by getting your emotions in check, getting the facts straight and having rehearsed your position then it is time to intervene. The entry point into a tough political conversation might sound something like this...

'Jerry, the facts are that the Genesis project is in more trouble than anyone will seem to admit and I want to resolve this situation for the good of the business, so let's have the difficult conversation about what is really going on behind the scenes and what we can do about it.'

Yes, one sentence; don't stop until you finish, but remember to draw breath!

What happens next is critical. We have handed Jerry a moral dilemma and he now has the choice to get honest or get gamey. His choice will help you determine what to do next. Be encouraged though that our experience is that this type of tough political confrontation can produce remarkable results, with many Machiavellian managers being coaxed back into more productive dialogue.

Notice how our strategy contains a reference to the needs of the business rather than the needs of the individual. This enables the conversation to move away from an adversarial 'you against me' engagement and invites dialogue about the business needs rather than personal needs. Removing the personal polarization provides a better invitation to Machiavelli to get productive; okay, he won't always take it, but we did at least provide him with the chance to do the right thing.

If Jerry takes the offer to co-operate then the situation moves forward productively. Should he decide to continue holding his adversarial position; then we need to retreat and continue working with our supporters. Retreating is not the same as admitting defeat. Retreating in the face of immovable force gives us the chance to regroup and try again. We can't and won't win every political battle we come across so knowing when to engage and when to retreat are key political skills. The bottom line is that your project may well be destined to failure. Even if you can turn it around, unless you are savvy the forces ranged against you will work even harder to make sure you fail.

One lady told us of her *Fall Guy* project through our website. Initially she thought it was her opportunity to show people what she was made of. She knuckled down, worked hard and started to make real progress in turning the project round. As she started to win, the Machiavellian types increased their efforts to create failure by withdrawing resources and starting rumours. In the end she resigned because she couldn't cope with the personal attacks. Believe it or not, she worked for a charitable organization!

In tackling this you need to use all your resources, build relationships and work hard to keep track of the adversaries and their tactics (which is why you should make sure and read about all the Dirty Tricks in this book). At the end of the day, as a minimum if you can demonstrate high skill levels in trying to do the right thing for the business, can remain calm and objective (even smile) and get to the end point with your integrity intact, this is probably going to be recognized by your key stakeholders. They will think twice about losing such a valuable resource.

THE POWER OF ...

REALLY GREAT QUESTIONS

For all of our antidotes you will notice we have created questions for you to ask. There is real value in adapting our generic questions and composing your own in advance so that they become specific and pertinent to your situation. Great questions are usually open and are positive in their intent; in other words, they are designed to be helpful and elicit quality information, rather than being adversarial and provocative. Firing closed questions that lead and limit their response makes Machiavelli even more guarded and defensive than usual. Really good questions are designed to raise awareness and understanding of the situation, to bring clarity to problem solving, not to provide 'gotcha' moments. The more good questions that we can ask Machiavelli, then the more that we leave them no place to hide in our negotiations, and the more that we are likely to discover about how they think and feel, and what their real intent is.

DEVELOPMENT
OPPORTUNITY

The tactic of motivating someone to take on a task, project or assignment they might reasonably refuse, by pretending it is a development opportunity.

Good managers use delegation as an effective means of developing skills, experience and self-confidence in those whom they manage and lead. A genuine development opportunity provides a stretching and testing task. The employee is provided with adequate support, encouragement, resources, information and authority. They are genuinely set up for success. It is the way in which delegation and empowerment were supposed to work, before the unscrupulous hijacked them for their own purposes.

Your internal radar for Dirty Tricks should have detected how Jerry sells Ben Project Genesis (Achilles) as a 'development opportunity'. *Development Opportunity* becomes a game when the 'opportunity' is really a cover-up position for some disingenuous dirty work emerging from the organizational shadows or sewers. Machiavellian managers and leaders play this game for any number of self-interested and disingenuous reasons ...

- An attempt to seduce people into feeling better about taking on an unpleasant project.
- To dump unwanted assignments on the unwary.
- To covertly increase the workload of another.
- To disguise their own incompetence or lack of skill.
- To avoid politically unfashionable projects.
- To demonstrate to others an apparent aura of modern, cutting-edge management style, embracing delegation and empowerment.

A variation of this game is when the *Development Opportunity* is used as a cover-up position for getting someone out of the way. This can range from secondment to resignation.

GAME STATS: DEVELOPMENT OPPORTUNITY

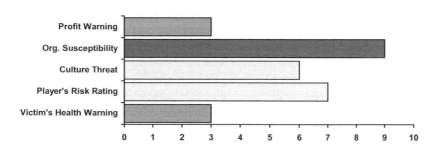

PROFIT WARNING 3/10 (OVERALL, WHAT RISK DOES THIS PRESENT TO THE BOTTOM LINE FOR THE ORGANIZATION?)
In isolation this is not too serious for the bottom line. However, beware of the effects of combining it with a trick like *Fall Guy*.

ORG. SUSCEPTIBILITY 9/10 (HOW PRONE IS AN ORGANIZATION TO THIS TYPE OF BEHAVIOUR?)
In the workshops we run, so many people have a cynical reaction to a *'Development Opportunity'*, it seems to us that this is so popular that the very meaning of the words are starting to change. Many euphemisms have lost their power though overuse. Tell 100 middle managers that you have a 'challenge' for them and we'd wager that greater than half would immediately recode that as a 'problem' heading their way!

CULTURE THREAT 6/10 (HOW DOES THIS AFFECT THE ORGANIZATION CULTURE, AND STAFF MORALE?)
Overuse in an organization will breed cynicism. As this takes hold, interest in development opportunities will wane and genuine chances to expand skills will start to pass by unrecognized. Beware also that when this trick is played, the victim will move between two extremes – delight and despair.

PLAYER'S RISK RATING 7/10 (HOW RISKY IS IT FOR THE PLAYER TO PLAY THIS DIRTY TRICK AND RISK EXPOSURE?)
The more a Machiavellian manager uses this tactic then the more it reduces in power. Team members get savvy to it quickly and Machiavelli will begin to wonder why the team doesn't seem to be interested in these delegated assignments. He will also be surprised at just how creative his team become at avoiding them.

VICTIM'S HEALTH WARNING 3/10 (WHAT RISK IS THE VICTIM PLACED UNDER WHEN THIS TRICK IS IN PLAY?)
Unless used in combination with other more dangerous games, this is a fairly tame one. Not only is it usually played with low impact assignments, they are often quite small. Once you've recognized the trick and learned the antidote it can be surprisingly easy to extricate yourself, unless you want to go to Luton of course!

THE ANTIDOTE: DEVELOPMENT OPPORTUNITY

Next time someone offers you a *'Development Opportunity'* and you are suspicious about their motives, experiment with some or all of the following smart questions. These will help you to determine if the opportunity is genuine or if it is just a game. Alternatively if we are a tad too late and you have already been 'opportunitied' then go back and enquire some more!

POWER QUESTIONS TO ASK ABOUT DEVELOPMENT OPPORTUNITIES
- What exactly is involved?
- What is the connection between this opportunity and my development plan?
- How does this move my development forward?
- How might this be a good move for the business?
- How might this be a good move for our customers?
- Why have I been identified for this?
- Who else was considered for this and why were they rejected?

- What was the thinking behind me taking this on?
- Why is this a good time for me to be pursuing this opportunity?
- What will the success criteria be?
- What timescales are we working to? How will we know when it is finished?
- What happens after this opportunity is finished?
- What impact will this have on my current workload and schedule?
- Which of my current priorities should I cancel to find room for this?
- What resources will be made available to me?
- How might this be relevant to my current work and career plan?
- What's in it for me?
- What's in it for you?
- What happens if I say 'thanks, but no thanks'?

These questions provide a quality control check for setting objectives; remember SMART[2]? If your boss can answer most of these, a SMART objective is within your grasp and this is unlikely to be a game. Depending on how your boss responds, you've got a number of options on what you say next:

- **Option 1:** 'Jerry, with the best of intentions, I'm going to take a risk. I have to say that this feels like a bit of knee jerk delegation. I want us to ensure that we get this right first time for everyone, so why don't we get more creative about our options and work together to make a better plan?'
- **Option 2:** 'Thanks for the opportunity Jerry, but no thanks.'
- **Option 3:** 'Jerry, I wonder why you are making this sound like a choice, when in fact this is not negotiable? I wonder why you couldn't just tell me directly that you just wanted me to take this assignment on? In future let's be more direct with one another.'
- **Option 4:** 'Thanks Jerry, I'll get straight down to work'

Whatever Jerry does next clearly signposts up what sort of a boss he is. You have given

---

[2] Specific, Measurable, Achievable, Relevant and Time scaled objectives.

him every chance of being assertive and straight in his delegation style. If he gets upset and continues to use this tactic, then at least you know what sort of an animal you have managing you and you are now forewarned.

THE POWER OF ...

GETTING OVER IT
Organizational politics is a fact of life; it is not going to go away however deeply you bury your head in the sand and hope that it will. Ostriches make very poor positive politicians. Sadly very few people get structured, professional help with managing organizational politics. However, help is at hand now from a number of professional and enlightened management development providers. According to a recent study by eminent researchers at Roffey Park, 46% of managers only learned political skills from watching others, so a little professional help is likely to go a long way, especially if the political skills they have been observing and learning are from Machiavelli. The more that we deny the existence of politics at work, the longer we maintain our ignorance and the more that we hand the advantage to the Machiavellian types who seek to exploit this outlook.

DIRTY TRICK NO. 3

KISS LIKE JUDAS

Declaring public support for an embattled project or individual, whilst privately plotting for change behind the scenes: 'I am more convinced than ever that Mark is the right person to lead the team through these difficult days.'

Sometimes as professional managers and leaders, we are not in a position to tell people on the team or in the organization the whole story. This could be due to legal or contractual obligations, under which circumstances these types of public pronouncements are a tough call, not a game. Often there are also genuine reasons of business strategy, timing etc. that inhibit full disclosure of the behind-the-scenes moves being made.

It becomes a Dirty Trick when someone is actively manoeuvring behind the scenes to make a personnel change, but lacks the courage or honesty to face the challenge and let people know where they really stand. The politically savvy amongst you will have detected on your political radar the telltale signs of this game, but sadly Ben, who was in a state of shock at the time, missed the apparent subtlety of what Jerry meant when he talked about how the MD had been publicly trumpeting Mark's achievements. *'Everyone believes that Mark has been doing a great job in difficult circumstances, the MD even said so at the last shareholders meeting...'*

Game connoisseurs will recognize that, strictly speaking, this is a variation on the theme because, as you will remember, Mark is the MD's son-in-law and is going to do quite nicely out of this game. Ben is going to lose out. *Kiss Like Judas* is usually reserved for a public declaration of support by a leader, whilst behind the scenes manoeuvring for replacement continues.

For those of you who watch professional sport, you will recognize the much dreaded 'vote of confidence' the director makes to the media, duplicitously suggesting full support to the embattled manager, coach or star player, immediately before the axe falls. And then, surprise surprise, the latest signing/new replacement is unveiled. The world of governmental politics is also littered with examples.

Why do leaders and managers feel the need to spin messages in this way? Do they not realize that these public statements have as much credibility as a government minister resigning to *'spend more time with my family'*? Do they not realize their people are by and large intelligent and are not so blinkered and credulous? Perhaps they lie because at some level they erroneously believe that the followers can't handle the truth and that some form of mass panic or collective hysteria will take place, therefore obfuscation is a better strategy.

As we remarked earlier, projects fail in organizations all the time and for any number of reasons. As the failure looms ever larger and the time runs out, everyone in the organization frequently knows who is responsible and what is really going on, so playing *Kiss Like Judas* becomes counter-productive as it generates a further lack of faith in the leadership. To the enlightened and astute it appears that the leadership have become increasingly desperate to hypnotize the entire workforce into believing that everything will be okay, provided everyone ignore reality and keep the faith. Unsurprisingly this Dirty Trick fans the flames and provides fodder for the cynics. The cost to the organization's emotional balance sheet is great. Cynicism, distrust and suspicion from the workforce toward corporate communications dramatically reduce leadership effectiveness.

The most obvious reason for the popularity of *Kiss Like Judas* is that often the person leading the very public, positive outpourings in support of some incompetent manager, is the same person who hired or appointed them to the project in the first place. Therefore their failure exposes the leader to 'reputation contamination through association with failure', which is an executive condition that leaders and managers are rightly afraid of! Sadly they frequently believe that this Dirty Trick will save them whilst they attempt to secretly sacrifice one *Fall Guy* and engage a replacement. The really bad news is that sometimes it works and they get away with it, at least in the short-term. Longer term credibility and integrity are however contaminated.

GAME STATS: KISS LIKE JUDAS

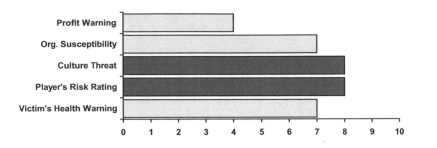

PROFIT WARNING 4/10 (OVERALL, WHAT RISK DOES THIS PRESENT TO THE BOTTOM LINE FOR THE ORGANIZATION?)
On its own this trick is probably not that damaging to the bottom line. What are lost are the beneficial effects of trust and positive effort to get the real issues dealt with for the benefit of the organization. Damage can escalate quickly if *Kiss Like Judas* is combined with other tricks.

ORG. SUSCEPTIBILITY 7/10 (HOW PRONE IS AN ORGANIZATION TO THIS TYPE OF BEHAVIOUR?)
It never ceases to amaze us just how much effort people will exert to avoid owning up to mistakes. Perhaps this is not so surprising because often when this trick comes into play, the senior powers have already invested significant time, effort and motivational speeches into the project. Perhaps its just habit!

CULTURE THREAT 8/10 (HOW DOES THIS AFFECT THE ORGANIZATION CULTURE, AND STAFF MORALE?)
This Dirty Trick is seriously damaging to the credibility of corporate communications and the directors or managers who sign the messages of 'spin' off. Once the ruse has been rumbled, cynicism grows alarmingly and genuine authentic communication is treated with suspicion.

PLAYER'S RISK RATING 8/10 (HOW RISKY IS IT FOR THE PLAYER TO PLAY THIS DIRTY TRICKS AND RISK EXPOSURE?)
The main worry here for players is personal credibility. Who do you think you are kidding? What does this tell everyone in the organization who actually knows what is going on? Do you think your staff are ignorant or will burst into tears if you are honest with them? Shame on you!

VICTIM'S HEALTH WARNING 7/10 (WHAT RISK IS THE VICTIM PLACED UNDER WHEN THIS TRICK IS IN PLAY?)
Risk levels depend on your personal involvement and type of organization. As we noted earlier, in professional sport, being 'kissed' means you are done for! Elsewhere, if you are being 'kissed' then reputation damage and 'career realignment' is just around the corner. If it is your manager being kissed, you may well be about to have a change at the top, and depending on your outlook, this may not be so bad.

IMPORTANT CAVEAT
Not all corporate communications are spin and this type of public 'kissing' can sometimes be genuine – no really, stop laughing over there at FA headquarters.

THE ANTIDOTE: KISS LIKE JUDAS

If you are a leader who uses this game, then you might like to reflect for a while about the longer term impact of using this strategy. Whichever way you want to rationalize it, the bottom line is that you are lying to your people. And, guess what? Our research suggests that they are seldom taken in by such tactics. The evidence suggests that at best all you have done is bought a little time for yourself at great expense on the emotional balance sheet.

Furthermore, this tactic serves to breed cynicism around your communications and damages your personal credibility and integrity. Also, what happens now that people in your organization are reading this book and know this strategy? Do you need any more reasons to stop?

Tackling a leader, who thinks that *Kiss Like Judas* is a good idea, is risky. It requires courage, and even if done skilfully it may still turn out to be a 'career decision' for whoever takes up the baton but gets their political intervention strategy wrong. In short, this is one of those games where you really have to want to intervene as an act of courage. The best advice emerging from our research and workshops is to choose your battles strategically, and we agree with this wholeheartedly. Even whistle blowers who publicly expose the duplicity of multinationals in the press can pay a high personal price, beyond losing their jobs.

We have however identified three best practice tactics for handling this trick proactively and positively. Before you act, read this book completely and do an audit on other tricks that could be in play. Then carefully consider the negative consequences for the organization if *Kiss Like Judas* continues. These thoughts will be an invaluable resource to draw on when you tackle the player.

1 Challenge in private, don't expose in public. Leaders who are playing this game are very unlikely to admit it publicly, so find a way of getting a more private word with them somehow. If you feel that you want to expose them publicly, then you are probably acting out of revenge when you could be acting for the common good. Be careful with that emotion!
2 When you meet with them ensure that you can find some way of helping them to save face and get out of this situation positively. Remember that they probably chose this game because they want to save face over a bad choice they made in the first place.
3 Help them come up with a better plan and more positive long-term strategy. Go into that meeting with at least three ideas for them to consider.

We also suggest that you might like to consider some appropriately tough and tactful political challenging to use in your meeting. In this context it might sound something like this ...

> 'Jerry, I suspect that you are uncomfortable with the way Project Genesis is being led and that it puts you in a tricky situation personally. Rightly or wrongly, no one seems too convinced about the old man's speech in support of Mark, and I want to get a better outcome for everyone, yes even the shareholders! I have some ideas I want to discuss for how to make the situation better for you.'

Now, we know that to some of you, this sounds pretty direct and tough. Well, yes it is, and it will probably need to match the conversational and thinking style of the person you are challenging. We know from the story that Jerry wears an outside persona of 'tough guy' so in order to influence him, matching him needs to be tough. Now, there is no guarantee that this will work, but our experience is that variations on this theme, which is designed to show concern rather than accusation and creativity rather than blame, gives you the best chance of success. Notice also the joke about the shareholders, which is intended to lighten the conversation and reduce the tension in the communication.

Even if you are not successful with your intervention it is quite likely that Jerry might still be impressed at the confidence and courage you demonstrated. Jerry is most likely to want a team with tough characters in his own image. You also signal to him the concern you have for both him and for the team, and you also get the satisfaction of knowing that you did the right thing, and that you did what you could in a very difficult situation.

If the leader reacts badly to your well-intentioned intervention, (and you know that you have acted with a clear heart and with skill and tact) then you have probably learned a valuable lesson about the type of leader or organization you are working in. Now it is your turn to decide what happens next

THE POWER OF ...

PROJECTION AND TRANSFERENCE

If you think that your boss or someone else has the power, and you feel power-less, think again. Sure the boss has power, but everyone working in the organiza-tion has power, especially you. Your known power sources probably come from your expertise, your skill with words and people, or perhaps you are a wiz with IT. However, what about all the power that is projected on to you by others, sources which you are not aware of? On our workshops we ask delegates where they think our power comes from even though they have only just met us. Without excep-tion they cite a wide variety of sources, which often have no basis in reality. They project this power onto us and we are happy to accept it. This type of power trans-ference happens all the time. Ask a trusted friend for their ideas about how you are perceived and what assumptions people make about your power.

CHAPTER TWO

THE

APPRENTICE

How could he leave Ben feeling down like that? Okay, perhaps Lewis had been a little rash to cast doubt in Ben's mind, but only a small slip. 'Listen Ben, whatever the reason is for Mark going off to Florida, you have now got an opportunity to make a name for yourself. If I were you I'd just get cracking and show them what you're made of.' With that Lewis sauntered off for a coffee, confident in the knowledge that Ben would soon be out of the way. He chuckled inwardly. What a sucker.

Sauntering was of course a practised art. Lewis had always thought rushing was particularly abhorrent. He had always regarded his self-control and fluidity of movement as a great asset. Even at school he had learned early that a smooth stroking back of his hair, with a nonchalant smile had given him a certain magnetism. The extent to which this self-impression was misguided in the harsh reality of Xennic had never been pointed out. The usual, carefully guarded reaction was 'what a creep'.

Slowing his pace, Lewis reflected on how upset he had been when Ben was appointed. He'd made all the right noises and carefully crafted his moves, the right moves. How could he have missed getting that job? It was beginning to dawn on him now. A smart move by Jerry perhaps?

Now that the Genesis game was in play, Lewis surmised that maybe, just maybe, there was method in their madness. Achilles was going down the tubes. Many of his friends – yes, he really did have some friends – had already managed to jump ship and he was certainly glad to be out of the way. It looked very much like the powers that be needed a scapegoat. Perhaps that was why Ben had beaten him to the job? His obvious talents were being saved for another day. On reflection there was plenty that he could have done to help Ben with Achilles and how he might go about saving both the project and himself, but then again ...

Why should he? His status as Jerry's protégé had been confirmed during a quiet tête-à-tête during a corporate function. Jerry looked upon him as a loyal supporter and saw real potential in him. The quantity of empty whisky bottles failed to register on Lewis's rather duller than usual senses on that particular occasion, but Jerry's words were now hardwired into his consciousness. Reflecting on this bolstered the belief that his moment of glory was approaching.

Because Lewis knew the 'way things work round here' there was lots of advice he could give Ben. But that wasn't his style, particularly if the movers and shakers had other plans. Wouldn't want to ruffle their feathers and threaten his own position, particularly if he was soon destined to get Ben's job.

'Guess they'll end up blaming it on a recruitment foul up and be able to take another shot at the HR director who seriously upset Jerry at a board meeting six months ago,' he concluded as he took the back stairs to the coffee lounge. He always preferred the stairs, particularly since they put that infernal camera in the lift. Lewis much preferred to stay in the quiet shadows where he could operate unobserved. Perhaps it was his unconscious mind attempting to conceal his hairstyle. He had explained it to himself that he needed the exercise to tone up his physique.

Pleased with his own sense of destiny, and impressed by his own grasp of what he thought was really happening, he entered the lounge. Certainly in Lewis's view a very civilized innovation to improve the workplace culture. To relax and talk shop over a coffee in armchairs was a definite motivator for Lewis and closely aligned to his sense of being.

Sarah Lees spotted him enter and started to make a beeline for him. She really was rather good. Whoever brought her into the business needed a medal. Not only was she excellent at her job, she was also quite stunning to look at. Before he had extracted his cappuccino from the machine, Sarah was at his side with a warm smile. 'Hi Lewis, I'm glad I caught you'.

'I'm very glad you caught me too' he leered. Forcing himself away from thoughts best left undisclosed, Lewis just managed to muster sufficient political correctness to continue 'What's on your mind Sarah?'

'Well, you know we've always had problems with the Customer Acquisition Process, whereby 1 in 5 need to be reworked; well, I've got an idea how we can rectify this and save approximately £300k per annum.' 'Go on, this sounds interesting' said Lewis, somehow managing to maintain eye contact and keeping his gaze from drifting elsewhere.

Sarah went on to outline her analysis of the problem, suggested a way of redesigning the process and how she calculated the large savings. Lewis was interested, very interested indeed. She also had a cracking idea with real potential and was actually asking him for help.

'Listen Sarah, it all sounds wonderful in concept, but frankly it's unlikely to work. First you've got the IT problems. Do you know how long it takes to get anything changed there, particularly now there is a change freeze on? Also, it's not likely to be a big priority for the business right now. I don't mean to be discouraging, but let me give it some thought and let you know. Sorry, gotta dash now ...' He considered his next move. Perhaps he could help Sarah's career some more, over dinner perhaps?

Anxious as ever to make a good impression, Lewis moved with uncharacteristic haste. Taking the lift he collected his thoughts. He needed to catch Jerry on his way back from the board meeting. The idea was good. Very good. In fact a sure-fire winner and something that was very much on the right agenda as well. Perhaps he could use this to get back in the spotlight whilst Ben was away in Luton. He could almost have been forgiven for the unconscious smirk as he pictured Ben struggling to remain motivated in Luton.

'Ah, Jerry old chap, need a quiet word ... it's quite important'. He paused for effect. 'How do you fancy saving £600k this year on one of the key issues we raised at the SAD over the weekend? Not only will it save you a bunch of money, but we'll also be able to reduce the headcount a little I think … interested?'

'I'm listening, but make it quick, Lewis.' Whilst Lewis steadied his pace and delivered his ten-minute attempt at an elevator pitch, Jerry's thoughts drifted.

Why oh why had he stupidly suggested to Lewis that he was his 'apprentice?' For God's sake, Lewis was far too slow. Jerry prided himself on setting a quick pace, and this seemed to pass unnoticed by Lewis. Did he not realize yet that you had to be a fast mover in this place? Xennic was not a place for people who ambled through life. You had to be a mover and a shaker. Make things happen fast. And here he was, rambling on about saving a paltry £0.6m when the company had to cover a £12m overspend? Xennic's Achilles heel!

But Lewis was useful. And had proved so in many ways. Very malleable and could be sent on errands to move forward Jerry's agenda. Because of his slow pace, this often lulled adversaries into a false sense of security. Ready in fact for Jerry to strike.

'… personally I think we need to redesign …' Jerry reached a conclusion in his own mind and interrupted Lewis mid-sentence. 'Listen Lewis, you know as well as I do that we need to focus on priorities. With Achilles, um, Genesis we need to recover quickly. I think your idea could have legs, but to get the attention it deserves it needs to be a million plus saving. Why don't you pull together a research team, complete a business case, do a simulation test, and build a case for me to consider taking forward. This will need a sound business case if it is going to fly. Good thinking though Lewis, I think it might work eventually.'

Lewis failed to notice the haste with which he was ushered out of Jerry's office, partly because he had drifted out on the memory of being his apprentice …

CHAPTER TWO: MENTORING INTERVENTION

Not all Dirty Tricks reside in the lofty heights of the executive office. Many are played out day after day in the numerous interactions at a more junior level. This chapter is typical of the type of interactions that occur around us all the time. Does it ring any bells?

We think you'll agree that the scenes played out in this chapter could and probably are happening around you now. However, as we expose more and more of these, you'll soon start to get a feel for what is really happening and the consequences of allowing it to continue, for you, your team and the organization.

Before we spell them out, reflect back on the story so far and consider your answers to the following coaching questions. Remember there are no right answers and they are provided to help you to start thinking about the way you behave in the work setting and to raise your political awareness and savvy.

- What image is Lewis trying to project? How could this be useful in organizational life?
- How would you have responded to Sarah's idea?
- What should Sarah have done differently?
- What do you think would have happened if Sarah had gone directly to Jerry?
- Would Sarah respond positively to an invite to dinner from Lewis?
- What are the negative consequences of exaggerating the potential savings from Sarah's idea?
- How does Jerry benefit from his relationship with Lewis?
- What benefits does Lewis get?
- Does their relationship work to the benefit of the business?
- Should having bad hair lead to disciplinary action?

Let us now turn our attention back to the Dirty Tricks illustrated here. If you've skipped forward already, shame on you. If you've already recognized them either you are a savvy individual or ... shame on you!

THE DIRTY TRICKS IN CHAPTER TWO

DIRTY TRICK NO. 4: BYSTANDER
Knowing that someone is in a problematic situation, but standing on the sidelines, doing nothing, when intervention is appropriate and would be helpful to the business.

DIRTY TRICK NO. 5: CREATIVE MAGPIE
Exaggerating involvement in the ideas and good work of others, or blatantly stealing them and hiding the originators' worthy contributions.

DIRTY TRICK NO. 6: TELL ME MORE
The tactic of delaying decisions or honest disclosure by requesting more work, research or data which often includes the efforts of others.

DIRTY TRICK NO. 4

BYSTANDER

Knowing that someone is in a problematic situation, but standing on the side-lines, doing nothing, when intervention is appropriate and would be helpful to the business.

This trick is the self-interested act of deliberately allowing someone else to drift towards failure, embarrassment or worse at a time when intervention was still possible. It is a strange political act whereby the persecutor actually does nothing! This trick is usually played by *Bystanders* for their personal profit, hoping to benefit from the failure of another, and is particularly easy to play since the *Bystander* is often out of the direct reporting structure and it is often easier to 'say nothing' than to help. The *Bystander* is a silent witness and usually finds that doing nothing is the easiest and most advantageous position. It is strange to regard doing nothing as a political strategy and the absence of action or behaviour, makes this Dirty Trick doubly hard to spot.

However, the politically astute will know that *Bystander*s often leave tell-tale signs if we can get close enough to them to ask their opinions. When we engage with them, the *Bystander* will usually do a quick mental stock-take of the advantages and disadvantages of intervention, but often choose a hasty exit or change of subject. As you may have noticed at the end of Chapter One, Lewis alerted Ben to the fact that Mark was the MD's son-in-law. Yet at the start of this chapter he quickly tries to cover his 'mistake' by motivating Ben to get cracking, to make a name for himself, and then quickly exits (as quickly as Lewis is ever likely to and still remain consistent to his sense of style). The *Bystander*'s quick exit is usually to avoid any follow-up questions that could be in the mind of the victim.

We also learned earlier on in this chapter that Lewis is withholding information and is in a position to help Ben, but has decided that Ben's failure is his just reward.

Projects and initiatives fail all the time. It's a fact. Yet when the axe eventually falls, not many people appear to be surprised, except perhaps the poor unfortunates who are directly involved. This is symptomatic of an organizational tendency to stand by. At the point of failure, a great deal of post disaster rationalization occurs as the *Bystanders* quickly emerge from the shadow side of the organization and pick over the tragedy. They avoid difficult and appropriate questions about why they just watched the emerging disaster (if these are in fact asked) with lame excuses such as 'it was none of my business', 'not my responsibility' or 'it's not my style to interfere, particularly when I have so much else on my plate'. Often you will see the *Bystanders* looking happiest on the day the project is pulled, frequently at their most energetic as the rumour mill and grapevine go into overdrive.

The reasons for taking this position are multiple and complex. However, you can strip away this complexity because at the end of the day, they will either not be damaged by the failure or might directly benefit. In Lewis's case, his logic is that with Ben out of the way on a doomed project, he is one step closer to success, or taking his job, which he believes was his by rights anyway. Sometimes fear can play a factor. To get involved in a difficult situation may expose an individual to scrutiny and challenge. They may end up tarnished and be linked with the ailing individual or project. Not a good career move many will reason.

GAME STATS: BYSTANDER

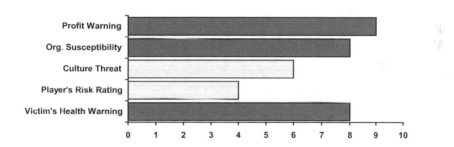

PROFIT WARNING 9/10 (OVERALL, WHAT RISK DOES THIS PRESENT TO THE BOTTOM LINE FOR THE ORGANIZATION?)
Apart from some petty moves, this trick is usually found when the stakes are highest. Although the project is doomed to fail, intervention still has the opportunity to protect the bottom line. A swifter end can save thousands. Marshalling creative talent to snatch victory from the jaws of defeat, or to look at innovative ways to salvage corporate value from the lessons are often overlooked in the emerging politicking[1].

---

[1] How many *Bystanders* watched Nick Leeson gamble away the fortunes of Barings Bank? How many *Bystanders* were silent witnesses to the collapse at Enron?

ORG. SUSCEPTIBILITY 8/10 (HOW PRONE IS AN ORGANIZATION TO THIS TYPE OF BEHAVIOUR?)
Human beings are programmed at birth to take the easiest route. When mixed with a strong selfish nature, or a score to settle, why rock the boat? It appears all too easy to lurk in the shadows as a *Bystander*!

CULTURE THREAT 6/10 (HOW DOES THIS AFFECT THE ORGANIZATION CULTURE, AND STAFF MORALE?)
This trick is difficult to see because we tend not to recognize doing nothing as a political strategy. The victims have plenty of other things to occupy their thinking time and the *Bystanders* lurk in the shadows doing nothing. As the stress rises their minds fail to spot the clues, and the potential sources of help. The cultural threat is really one whereby failure is allowed to happen too often. This creates a general drag on staff morale but not a haemorrhage.

PLAYER'S RISK RATING 4/10 (HOW RISKY IS IT FOR THE PLAYER TO PLAY THIS DIRTY TRICK AND RISK EXPOSURE?)
This is low risk because the chances of being caught in the act are minimal. Even when they are caught, it is relatively easy to feign innocence or claim to be not responsible and then latterly to appear to offer help.

VICTIM'S HEALTH WARNING 8/10 (WHAT RISK IS THE VICTIM PLACED UNDER WHEN THIS TRICK IS IN PLAY?)
With others making personal decisions about the problem the victim is facing, the indicators warn that this situation could get very bad indeed. This risk may be aggravated by other tricks being played behind the scenes to steer the project closer to failure, or to amplify the problems of the victim to carefully selected ears (note that this does however heighten the risk of exposure). With potential sources of help, often quite capable and influential, standing by, watch out!

THE ANTIDOTE: BYSTANDER

This is so easy to play. To give you some insights into the mind of the player, think of a difficult issue that you either are, or could be a *Bystander* for? Be honest with yourself in the safety of this book and explore the situation by asking yourself the following questions about the issue:

- What good reason do I have for not getting involved?
- What would it cost me personally by getting involved?
- What is the cost to my colleagues, clients and customers if I take the *Bystander* position?
- What is the cost to the business if I do not intervene?
- To what extent am I happy to see my colleague(s) fail? Why is that?
- What are my colleagues expecting of me in this situation?
- What is the organization expecting of me in this situation?
- How likely is it that I am being subtly manipulated into intervening?
- How will I feel when this project finally fails?
- If I was to intervene what is the worst that can happen?
- If I am honest with myself, and true to my values, is the *Bystander* position justified?

These questions are designed to test out your position and check to make sure that you are aligned with your values. Any disconnection between your actions and your values is likely to cause stress and discomfort. Therefore these questions may prompt you to do the right thing for your customers, your colleagues, your organization and most importantly of all, you.

Okay relax; let us now turn our attention to how to handle someone else playing this trick. The critical aspect is recognition. Unless you can see this, it is impossible to handle. Yet if you do the benefits can be significant.

Because this trick is usually in play when you are in a tight spot, get into the habit of noticing your stress levels about an issue you are working on. As soon as you recognize that things could be getting a little hot, try to stand back for a moment and ask yourself:

- Who is being less helpful than I would expect?
- Who might be able to help me in this situation, but is not?
- Is anybody being evasive or making obscure statements about the situation?
- Has anybody started to help but then backed off?
- Who is suggesting this is a difficult situation but not offering any constructive advice or help?

Depending on the nature of your situation or project, you could have any number of *Bystanders*. You need help so rather than trying to pick on the closest, prioritize those who you believe could be most helpful, or dangerous to you. When you have selected those to tackle, for each one consider –

- Why do I suspect they are *Bystanding*?
- What reasons could they have for taking this position?
- How will they benefit if I fail?
- How could they benefit from helping me?
- What is the worst that could happen if I tackle them?

When you have decided to confront a *Bystander*, try to adopt a positive attitude and resist the temptation to accuse. Your best chances of extricating yourself from the difficult situation you find yourself in, is to enlist help and support, not create or reinforce enemies.

POWER QUESTIONS TO ASK THE BYSTANDER
- I couldn't help but notice you think I'm in a hole here; can you help me understand your thinking?
- You dropped a hint the other day that people are opposed to this project. Can you be more specific?

- What are your reservations?
- What do you envisage is likely to happen here?
- What positive outcomes can you see?
- What steps should I take to bring things back under control?
- What would your advice be?
- Who is really opposed to this project?
- If you could help, how would the organization benefit?
- What would you gain from helping?

At the end of the day remember, everyone is entitled to free choice. If they are still intent on remaining a *Bystander*, seek another route to get the help you need and deserve. Remember also that a *Bystander* might be hoping to profit personally from your failure so be on your guard should you decide to engage with them. Another useful part of your strategy should be to identify key players and stakeholders close to the *Bystander* as they might be worth appealing to because of the leverage they might be able to provide.

One of the keys to successful positive politics is to work most closely with those whom you trust and are in agreement with, to develop political momentum. Time invested with these allies is usually time better spent than in attempting to convert *Bystander*s to the cause.

THE POWER OF ...

SECOND POSITION THINKING
The great American management guru Stephen Covey believes that you should 'seek first to understand then to be understood'. Before taking your assertive action and tackling Machiavelli, spend some time considering the situation from their viewpoint. What is compelling them to act in such manipulative ways? What external pressures might be driving their need to manipulate and use Dirty Tricks? What other options have they ignored or cannot see? This second position think-

ing can greatly inform your strategy and your chances of success. This way we get a new insight into what is going on for them and what might be driving their need to behave in such manipulative ways. When we talk about how difficult their situation must have been, or how hard their decision was, we demonstrate our consideration and signal our positive intent. It can also be helpful to extend this process to consider the outlooks that other *Bystanders* or stakeholders might have, especially if they are likely to get involved at some stage. How does this situation seem from their vantage point?

DIRTY TRICK NO. 5

CREATIVE MAGPIE

Exaggerating involvement in the ideas and good work of others, or blatantly stealing them and hiding the originators' worthy contributions.

The *Creative Magpie* comes in many varieties. The lesser-spotted magpie flies around collecting ideas, data and proposals from others. These are then fed up to a higher authority but presented as the magpie's own work. The more vicious variety (the vulture magpie) listens to great ideas and then demoralizes its victim by suggesting the idea is awful and is destined to the waste bin, particularly 'from someone in your position'. Having ensured that the idea will not pop up via another route, they then take the shiny new idea to the top table confident in the glory that will follow. No prizes for working out which variety Lewis was born into.

Whichever variety you discover, the bottom line is that they are stealing. Often we find that their rationale is that the idea will not go anywhere unless their superior skills or position is behind it. Sometimes this is shared with the victim. To add insult to injury, the victim can also be asked to add further time and effort and the theft only happens in the last moment.

One colleague told us of her experience of this. After spending several weeks putting together a talent retention strategy, her boss thanked her for her efforts and then, before emailing it to the HR director, he replaced her name with his own. That was the extent of the effort he put into the project. She only discovered this after it was circulated to a wider audience following a steering committee meeting to which she had not been invited. Ironically, her talents were soon being deployed by another organization. Oh, and the magpie has also moved on to premature retirement!

At the heart of a magpie is a seriously insecure person. Someone who perhaps lacks the skills needed to perform to an acceptable level, or is seriously concerned about needing to look good but is unable to back this up with genuine high performance. They also seem to have missed the management development module on how to get the best out of other people and that you can get serious benefit from being recognized as someone who can develop others and push them forward.

The sad fact about this trick is that it breeds demotivation very quickly, particularly when exercised on the lower ranks who often feel powerless to act. After all, a magpie doesn't rob an eagle's nest! The rot quickly sets in and the ideas and energy dwindle. What is the point if I'm never going to get recognized here? With the organizational imperative increasingly becoming 'innovate or die' all businesses should wake up to the drain this trick can have on the talent that they have worked so hard to recruit and develop.

GAME STATS: CREATIVE MAGPIE

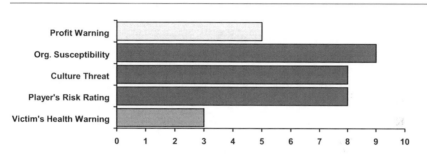

PROFIT WARNING 5/10 (OVERALL, WHAT RISK DOES THIS PRESENT TO THE BOTTOM LINE FOR THE ORGANIZATION?)
Sadly, the overall impact on the organization, particularly in the short-term is low, since at least great ideas are being moved forward. Longer term however, the impact gets worse as the ideas start to dry up, and the re-recruitment costs start to rise.

ORG. SUSCEPTIBILITY 9/10 (HOW PRONE IS AN ORGANIZATION TO THIS TYPE OF BEHAVIOUR?)
With the pressure on for individuals to prove their value to the bottom line, the temptation to play this trick at some level is high. Particularly amongst the lower ranks, most of us have been visited by a magpie.

CULTURE THREAT 8/10 (HOW DOES THIS AFFECT THE ORGANIZATION CULTURE, AND STAFF MORALE?)
If this trick is widespread, the culture is likely to be much less innovative than it should be. Since the culture is 'the way we do things round here' this trick will soon transform one of the norms to 'have an idea, see it pinched'.

PLAYER'S RISK RATING 8/10 (HOW RISKY IS IT FOR THE PLAYER TO PLAY THIS DIRTY TRICK AND RISK EXPOSURE?)
This trick is one of the easiest to recognize, particularly after the event. Therefore it represents a high risk to the player as they will soon get a reputation and their staff will soon learn to do things differently. Also the player risks a downturn in productivity as morale drops. This can quickly give them even more things to worry about.

VICTIM'S HEALTH WARNING 3/10 (WHAT RISK IS THE VICTIM PLACED UNDER WHEN THIS TRICK IS IN PLAY?)
Actually low risk but very annoying. So you fail to get recognized for the idea or hard work. Often the theft gets exposed and recognition may follow. It also has the interesting twist of making the magpie more dependent on you, raising your personal power in the relationship. Another interesting aspect is that the magpie seldom really understands your idea fully and fails to articulate it convincingly.

THE ANTIDOTE: CREATIVE MAGPIE

How you deal with the magpie depends on when you catch them. If you want to catch them whilst they are still in the nest, try 'resist and insist'. However, if they have flown before you discovered your loss you have time to consider your strategy carefully and use 'vaccination'.

RESIST AND INSIST
Surprisingly, in this strategy it is not critical that you have identified them as a magpie,

nor that you have reason to distrust their motivations. If they are a magpie, using this tactic will put them under some serious pressure. Yet don't worry if you haven't got a magpie in front of you because it is highly likely if your tone is right that they will respect you regardless.

When they suggest that they will 'take it from here', politely resist and insist that you take responsibility for presenting your own work. Let them know that you are confident enough in your own abilities to take it further, and that you want to see it through. Thank them for their support, interest and contribution, but continue to resist and insist that you need this learning opportunity. These opportunities can be few and far between and you deserve to test yourself, and if you pass this up, who knows when you might get another go. Gently resist and insist that you be allowed to stand or fall by your own hard work and talent. After all, no one knows as much about this project as you do, so who better than you to take it to the next stage?

In some circumstances you might need to acknowledge that they have the authority to insist that they take it forward on your behalf ('interns are not allowed at board meetings'). However you still have the right to be tenacious with resisting and insisting that you should have this opportunity to present your work. This approach signals clearly to the magpie how you want to manage things, and provided that throughout you remain calm, assertive and polite whilst resisting and insisting, you increase the chance that the magpie will get the message and leave your nest alone! Should they resist and insist back, then the following smart questions might prove helpful ...

POWER QUESTIONS TO ASK A MAGPIE
- What will you do with the more difficult technical questions they will have?
- What would be the cost to you of not being able to answer those questions?
- What would be the cost to you of them not liking this report/project/idea?
- What makes you think that I might not present this project as effectively as you?
- What will it take to convince you that I'm the best person to present this?
- Don't get me wrong Lewis, but what puts you in a better position than me to present this work?
- Why is presenting my work (to the board, steering group etc.) so important to you?

- What is behind this rule of not allowing interns to board meetings?
- What do you say we become the first to challenge that rule?

If you fail to get your way, don't fail to be clear about their reasons.

VACCINATION
If you find that your work has already been stolen, particularly if it is by a serial offender, you'll need to consider carefully the merits of tackling it. Whilst, without doubt, it is highly frustrating and demoralizing, weigh carefully the real damage that it is causing you. There could be other ways of avoiding this without risking the relationship by confronting the issue. At the end of the day, you're likely to continue working with or for the magpie for some time to come.

Overall we advocate assertive handling of the situation. Remember the benefits you can gain from fair recognition, not only to your career but also your development and enthusiasm for the place you work in. How much more confident will you feel when you have successfully stopped the rot? What else could you do with your increased confidence?

To apply the vaccine, firstly find the evidence. Check any facts very carefully. Do not rely on anecdotal whisperings by the coffee machines. The legal system has very good reason for checking the evidence so take heed. When you are ready, meet with the magpie and share the evidence. Do this in the spirit of enquiry at least initially. Depending on the nature of the crime, it may be advisable to give them the benefit of the doubt and suggest that it's probably a misunderstanding, but 'I'm sure you can see how it looks?'

At this point if you have presented a strong case you are likely to meet some excuses. Don't bother with them. Quickly move on instead to how it made you feel. But remember that this is probably going to be uncomfortable for the magpie to handle. Not only is he being exposed, but you are also sharing emotions. Because of this, closing with some pre-prepared positive suggestions will help. Usually these get seized on and taken seriously.

Throughout all of these transactions with the magpie it is vital to manage your emotions. The last thing you need is a stand-up row that ends with damage to your integrity and credibility, but at the same time you need to let the manager know you are displeased. The magpie may well consider it to be some sort of moral victory that offsets their poor performance if you 'lose it' in the meeting, but they retain their cool. Our behaviour and language need to describe the facts, our disappointment, and what we expect from our working relationships. Getting angry hands them the moral high ground and provides the perfect excuse for them to continue the game ...

'Calm down Sarah, this is the sort of emotional outburst that I was concerned about. Imagine if you had spoken like that to the directors.'

Most people who put this into practice are surprised at the results. This is particularly effective if you have been able to remain calm, have clear evidence and positive suggestions to move the relationship on. Having said that, even if it does not go as well as you think initially, the magpie will be more careful in future and will certainly think twice before stealing from you again!

THE POWER OF ...

PROTECTING BRIDGES
It is highly likely that the person you want to confront about their gamey ways is important to you in some way. It is also likely that in the future you may have to work together again, so be careful not to do permanent damage when you intervene. Burned bridges help no one. Part of your strategy needs to consider how you will enable the relationship to move towards a more authentic footing. Think through ways in which you can enable both of you to save face. Remember, relationships and results are connected, so we need to use our creative skills to ensure that at the critical point in the conversation, we have options for both parties to move forward. With options we advise you to have planned at least three

good ways to move the situation forward for maximum flexibility. In the absence of a WIN/WIN solution, then going for 'no deal' is always better than increasing manipulation or pretence. We might then become opponents of each other, but at least we know where we stand and avoid becoming adversaries. In every political encounter, work hard at keeping the bridges open.

TELL ME MORE

The tactic of delaying decisions or honest disclosure by requesting more work, research or data which often includes the efforts of others.

It is of course vital that before making key decisions, appropriate research is conducted, and that decisions are based on sound data and evidence. It is also true that many managers have a risk-averse way of coping with the complexity that organizational life throws at them, and as a result they have developed an almost insatiable appetite for data on which to base their decisions. This is their thinking style or decision-making profile, and frustrating though it may be if you have a more intuitive decision-making approach yourself – and are unlucky enough to report to them – it is not a political game or resistance strategy, just a difference of style.

Tell Me More only becomes a game when the manager has no real intention of taking the idea forward but lacks the integrity or assertiveness to explain why openly and honestly. Perhaps they feel that they don't have the time right now to explain to us the reasons why they cannot support our idea. Perhaps they are concerned that we will not be able to handle the rejection when they say no to our request. Or perhaps they are laying the groundwork for playing *Creative Magpie* by getting us to do the legwork before they steal the credit! The bottom line is that instead of being honest about their thinking and reasoning, they take a position where they appear to be supportive whilst at the same time are really saying 'no'. They use an apparently professional request for data to resist, delay, deflect or sabotage the idea.

They resist (indirectly) by asking for more and more facts and information to support the proposal. The manager's apparent stance is that there is not yet enough information to make the right decision. The reality is that there will probably never be enough information to convince them and they are resisting. They are hoping the suggestion will eventually go away, that the other party will eventually get distracted or diverted by more pressing priorities or that they will get the message that the manager is just not interested.

In our little story Jerry has more pressing problems to deal with. He doesn't seem to have the interest or time to focus on what Lewis is presenting. Lewis is also too wrapped up in the idea to recognize the clues. Never mind Lewis.

One client recently explained that this tactic was rife in his organization. Rather than act with integrity, directors preferred to put up a smoke screen and wait for the decision to go away. The net effect of this was that a huge amount of time and resources was being consumed with activities that were going nowhere. Interestingly this hit on the bottom line has been quantified by some research in the UK, which found that 'managers spend £12.3bn in time on activities that are going nowhere'[2].

GAMES STATS: TELL ME MORE

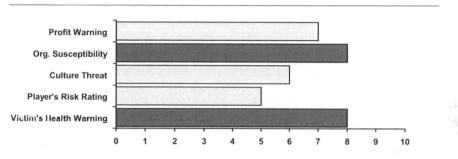

PROFIT WARNING 7/10 (OVERALL, WHAT RISK DOES THIS PRESENT TO THE BOTTOM LINE FOR THE ORGANIZATION?)
With regard to profits, the major problem this presents is a drag on management productivity. This could of course compound into competitive disadvantages, which over time could threaten the very survival of the organization. However, in the main the really important ideas get through to implementation.

ORG. SUSCEPTIBILITY 8/10 (HOW PRONE IS AN ORGANIZATION TO THIS TYPE OF BEHAVIOUR?)
This trick is so easy to play because of the cloak of clear business logic. Of course the facts need to be right and the case proven. To short-sighted managers the world over, this appears to be the quickest way to move on to their other interests rather than spend time explaining why the answer is 'no'.

---

[2] The SCQuARE Report 2004

CULTURE THREAT 6/10 (HOW DOES THIS AFFECT THE ORGANIZATION CULTURE, AND STAFF MORALE?)
Generally in our experience the culture seems embedded with this trick so that it really is 'the way we do things round here'. It often goes unchallenged and it is accepted as a fact of life. However, beware the small, rapidly growing company that quite rightly needs to add more rigorous processes to support growth. This can all too easily usher in a culture of '*Tell Me More*'.

PLAYER'S RISK RATING 5/10 (HOW RISKY IS IT FOR THE PLAYER TO PLAY THIS DIRTY TRICK AND RISK EXPOSURE?)
Not too risky for the player because of the easy excuses and unaware victims. If exposure does occur they can often wriggle out without too much risk. Perhaps the greatest risk facing the player is that of the drain on resources needed to deliver the results required by the organization. This makes it increasingly difficult for them to justify their position because they are squandering their people's time.

VICTIM'S HEALTH WARNING 8/10 (WHAT RISK IS THE VICTIM PLACED UNDER WHEN THIS TRICK IS IN PLAY?)
This can really hurt. If you have been subjected to this Dirty Trick, as we suspect you have, cast your mind back over the amount of time, energy and resources it took before you realized the idea was not going to happen. Add to this the potential damage to work/life balance as you struggle to get your project accepted whilst also having to deliver on all your other objectives as well. This can ultimately lead to burn-out and failure if you let this carry on too long.

THE ANTIDOTE: TELL ME MORE

Each manager has their own preferred way of working and operating and as we mentioned earlier, sometimes we work with a manager who has a very slow, analytical decision-making style. Frustrating as this may be, this is not a game, just their way of coping. The challenge is to determine at what stage it passes from being good professional practice into a manipulative and time-wasting game. Being trapped in a game of *Tell Me More* is like the film *Groundhog Day*, where despite your best efforts, there seems that nothing can be done to move the situation on.

If you suspect that your manager is using *Tell Me More* as a gamey form of resistance, try some or all of the following smart questions as a start point. The responses you get should give you a big clue about the extent to which the manager really supports your idea or project.

POWER QUESTIONS TO ASK THE MANAGER
- What will it take for you to be absolutely convinced this is a good project?
- What is the probability that this project will be signed-off? Can you explain your thinking?
- What specific criteria will I need to present to you?
- How much time and resource should I direct at this project?
- What do you see as the immediate benefits/pitfalls of this project?
- What is the possible impact on you if this project goes ahead?
- What personal involvement and contribution are you prepared to make?
- What are you not telling me about your reaction to this proposal?
- Who else should I consult with or involve at this stage?
- How much time/effort should I devote to this?
- What reaction will this project get from other parts of the business?
- How do you feel about what I have proposed?
- What cut-off date (the date by which if I have not convinced you, we will agree to drop it) should we set for the extra research?
- When will we know that it is time to pull the plug on this one?
- What is stopping you from giving a 'yes' right now?

You will notice that most of the above questions focus on the project in hand, therefore consider probing outside of this project for more clues. For instance:

- What other projects are competing for airtime?
- How does this proposal compare with them?
- What should I stop doing to create room for this extra research?

All of the above needs to be delivered with a polite and assertive tone of voice if we are to encourage the manager into a more productive dialogue. Control of our body language and gestures will be critical if we are to signal good intent, rather than adversarial positioning.

We want to encourage you to confront this game because it can be responsible for a huge hit on the bottom line, affect organizational efficiency and effectiveness and damage trust and co-operation. By intervening in this game you will at least signal your political awareness and savvy and leave the clear message that you are nobody's fool. Remember to act calmly and assertively.

THE POWER OF ...

IDEAS OVER ACCUSATIONS

You need to do more than be listened to, heard and understood when you confront an adversary. You need to ensure that there is a productive way forward at the end of it. Ensure when planning your intervention strategy, that you have plenty of ideas about how you can improve the situation and move things forward. The more ideas and options you have the better. The eminent Transactional Analyst Julie Hay taught us that three options are required to create genuine choice in these situations – one is a directive, two offers a dilemma, but only three options create real choice. Creativity and flexibility is key. Helping the other person see new ways forward increases your chances of success, invites them into more productive thought and dialogue and increases the likelihood of finding a new solution which will be acceptable to both of you.

CHAPTER THREE

COMMUTING TO (NO)WHERE?

Driving around the Luton one-way system for what seemed like the eighth time, lost, in torrential rain and with no sign of the turning he was looking for, Ben was beginning to wonder what he had done to deserve this. Apart from John Hegley, Eric Morecambe and a dodgy football team, what did Luton have to offer? Hanna had insisted that despite this suspect career move, the family would stay put and that Ben would have to commute. Now, looking out between sweeps of the windscreen wipers at the grey, shabby buildings, he realized that Hanna was right. Working in hell was one thing, but living here ...

Finally arriving at the Xennic outpost, Ben walked into reception. At least there were no revolving doors here. He spent the morning being processed by HR, IT and Security and at 11.30, no sooner than he was safely installed in his office he was summoned to a meeting with his boss.

Across the floor, Surrinder Patak's office was only a slightly grander affair than his own compact and bijou goldfish bowl, and compared most unfavourably with the splendour that was Jerry's domain. Patak herself, however, was warm and welcoming, offering handshakes and refreshments. Once past the initial welcomes and rituals, she steered the conversation on to activities in the London office.

'You know that Jerry and I go back some way?' No, Ben did not know that there was a connection between them.

'Oh yes, he's done some great work over the years. Taken many of my ideas and yet some would say we are old sparring partners. Many times in the past I have had to bail him out.' Ben did not know this, and frankly didn't much care. He had a mountain of work on his desk and wanted to get stuck in.

'I have watched his star in the ascendancy from this safe distance, but all stars burn out sometime.' The conversation was now taking a wilfully metaphysical turn that was as baffling as it was irritating.

'The higher they climb the harder they fall, do you know that expression Ben?' Ben nodded mutely, still unsure where she was going with this.

'And I wonder who will be there to catch him when he falls? Ben, tell me, how did you find Jerry?' Ben wanted to quip that you didn't find Jerry, rather you spent most of your time avoiding the ogre, but fortunately his diplomatic skills kicked in.

'I always found him to be very, er, direct.'

'Exactly, direct, like a bull in a china shop.' She then followed with a look, which suggested they were now fellow conspirators. Ben was working hard to navigate a way through these appalling mixed metaphors.

'Well I wouldn't say that exactly ...'

'Sledgehammer to crack a nut, perhaps?' These metaphors were now getting out of control.

'I wouldn't say that either ...'

Patak sighed, smiled and tried again using a different approach.

'Ben, do you like Jerry?' Surprised and confused Ben mumbled something inaudible and looked decidedly uncomfortable. Surrinder smiled. 'Ben, I know how things work in the London office, but understand that here in Luton we look out for each other in a spirit of comradeship and co-operation.'

Ben relaxed a little. 'Great, I am really looking forward to working with the team on the challenges ahead.'

Patak ignored him. 'So everyone on this team needs to know where their priorities and loyalties reside.'

Ben picked up on what he thought was the message. 'Good, because I wanted to talk to you about the immediate priorities for the project. I have not had a chance to decide where to start, so any advice would be most welcome.'

The conversation stalled and Ben was unsure why. They were not connecting as Ben had hoped. They looked at each other across the desk. The moment was broken by an interruption from the PA calling Patak to her next meeting.

Turning her attention back to Ben she said 'Yes, this meeting is perhaps a little early, so go away and do your prioritizing and we'll pick up this conversation again a bit later.'

She picked up her Palm Pilot and a few papers before turning back to him with her closing remarks. 'Ben, I am delighted that you have joined our team. I want to offer you all the support you need, so the quicker you get "on side" the better. I want to ensure that you are a big success here and get the rewards you deserve. So get with the programme, do good work, and who knows, you may even eclipse Jerry's star. Remember that Mark is now working in Florida, so let us both hope that Luton is now your land of opportunity.'

Ben stepped out of the office and out of the building in search of both lunch and time to think. Aside from her metaphors, Ben's first impression was favourable. She seemed big on, 'comradeship and co-operation' which certainly made a change. She seemed to have his best interests at heart and had made some encouraging suggestions about his bright future once he had got 'on side', whatever that meant. Clearly she was behind many of Jerry's successes, which seemed important to her.

Having finished his sandwich, Ben ambled into a bookshop to kill time. He found himself in the Business and Management section. He wondered who on earth found time to read all this guff. Moreover, who had the wherewithal to write such rubbish in the first place? Ben felt that these books were a world of conflicting ideas, peddled by snake oil salesmen. He picked up one on office politics and flicked through it, but quickly put it down again. '*Office Politics*, who reads this trash?' The woman standing next to him glanced in his direction and Ben had one of those, 'did I say that out loud', moments.

Back at the office his first visitor was Russell Bromley-Clark, a wise old owl who wanted to discuss Ben's ideas for Genesis. Ben took the opportunity to gently sound out Russell about Surrinder. Russell, feeling sorry for the poor lad, volunteered the fact that she and Jerry would be better described as mortal enemies. There was a strong rumour that things got so bad at one stage that Surrinder had even threatened a discrimination case against Jerry, but the whole thing had been covered up. 'Be warned Ben, Surrinder is gunning for Jerry at every opportunity.'

He now viewed his earlier, 'not quite on the same page here are we' conversation with Surrinder a little differently, but still he did not attach too much importance to it. Ben was just focused on delivering results and getting down to business, proving that he could rise to the 'development opportunity' that he had been handed.

At the end of the week Ben had his next meeting with Surrinder. He outlined the lack of strategic direction with Genesis to date, presented a damage limitation plan to cover the short-term and made a strong case for new timescales and refunding. Whilst he was not exactly expecting applause for his good work, he was totally taken aback by her response.

'Ben, there is no way I can let you present this plan as it stands at the next Strategic Away Day.'

'What? But I thought ...'

'Ben, you have had all week to get "on side".'

Ben fumbled through his confusion 'But I thought you wanted priorities? I thought you wanted to turn this project around?'

'Perhaps you are not as bright as your Saville and Holdsworth results suggest.'

'I still don't get it.'

'If you take this plan, as it stands, to the next SAD it will be career suicide, for both of us.'

Ben was appalled. What was going on?

'Come on Ben, I have been around long enough to know that JB will never support this plan.'

'Who's JB?'

'JB, the MD. Don't you even know that yet?' Surrinder paused to glance at the ceiling.

Ben quietly asked why he would not support this plan.

Surrinder had heard enough. It was time to get Ben 'on side'.

'Listen Ben, bottom line, no one gives a damn about project Genesis being a success. Everyone is resigned to its failure; however there is huge political capital to be gained in the short-term as it crashes.'

Ben rocked on his heels. 'Are you suggesting that I am wasting my time? Why am I here if everyone is resigned to failure?'

'Get a grip, Ben.' Surrinder was calm but not smiling. 'Jerry's plan is to wash his hands of the mess he created with Genesis, and I don't think his "contribution" should go unnoticed. Get it now?'

Ben was appalled. This was a major political battle and he was caught in the middle.

'But this is a huge waste of time and money,' protested Ben.

'Well at least you got that bit right.'

'But what does all this have to do with the MD?'

'Ben, there is more going on here than meets the eye. You need to trust me on this one that JB will never go for your plan as it stands; however, I have some suggestions.'

Ben felt hugely uncomfortable. He still had no idea what was wrong with his plan. Surrinder paused, sighed and then continued.

'Believe me Ben, dealing with me will be much easier than having to present to the MD directly. If you think Jerry is an ogre, wait until you have dealt with the big boss himself. Now, I have ideas for a few changes here and there, and then I think JB might give us the green light.'

Surrinder didn't say it, so Ben, in a fit of frustration, said it for her.

'And drop Jerry right back in the brown stuff at the same time?'

Surrinder sat back and smiled.

Ben was speechless and did not feel much like smiling. Once again he remembered what a colleague had told him: 'Being good is never going to be good enough, Ben.'

CHAPTER THREE: MENTORING INTERVENTION

Oh dear, poor Ben. Luton would have been bad enough without what he found in the office. Clearly he is having a tough time politically in his new role. Lots of mixed messages. Who can he trust?

   As with our other chapters, before we analyze this latest episode, and expose and explore the next three Dirty Tricks, treat yourself to a brief time out for some one-to-one political coaching with us. Ask yourself the following questions to check the levels of political intelligence.

- What should Ben have done differently in his first meeting with Surrinder?
- If you were sat on his shoulder in the second meeting with Surrinder, what would you have whispered?
- What options does Ben now have?
- Does Luton really deserve its accolade as 'Britain's Worst Town'[1]?
- What actions should Ben be setting up with regard to Genesis?
- How would you manage the competing forces of Jerry and Surrinder?
- What has really been going on behind the scenes?
- Are all management consultants snake oil salesmen?

Having reflected on the above, you are now ready to embark on the next part of our tour of Dirty Tricks in the workplace. If you have been following the story with your political radar switched on then you are likely to have detected the telltale clues which point the way toward the next three games we are going to expose and explore. Once again, if you have identified them correctly then you are indeed a politically astute and savvy individual, congratulations. If you are unsure, unwilling or confused then read on.

---

[1] *Crap Towns II: The Nation Decides* by Sam Jordison and Dan Keiran 2004

THE DIRTY TRICKS IN CHAPTER THREE

DIRTY TRICK NO. 7: INDIRECTLY YOURS
Hiding a view or belief by using indirect, obscure and confusing communication in order to tempt or fool someone into declaring their own position first.

DIRTY TRICK NO. 8: JAM TOMORROW
Making vague promises of future rewards to encourage people to take on unpleasant assignments, put in more effort, or take greater risks.

DIRTY TRICK NO. 9: GUARDIAN ANGEL
The tactic of implying friendly support, whilst at the same time suggesting that there are other more powerful people to answer to, who will be much tougher, unless co-operation is quickly forthcoming.

INDIRECTLY YOURS

Hiding a view or belief by using indirect, obscure and confusing communication in order to tempt or fool someone into declaring their own position first.

Indirect communication is everywhere in organizational life, and the game of *Indirectly Yours* is endemic. The political pressures that surround us can invite us into avoiding risk and controversy at every turn, leading us into being watchful and wary. This becomes noticeable in our communication style as we hedge our bets and leave escape routes if the tide turns against us.

In our story we are witness to a relatively mild form of *Indirectly Yours* when Surrinder gently sounds out Ben on any loyalty he may have towards his old boss Jerry. She carefully presents both support and opposition for Jerry, but neither directly. This leaves Ben with a confusing choice, which also appears a little irrelevant in his haste to work on the priorities. She seems satisfied with the result. Ben missed the significance of this obtuse conversation. He also missed with his plan at the end of the week; missed by a mile.

People use *Indirectly Yours* to drop hints, suggestions and loaded remarks in the hope that the other person will somehow figure out what they are deliberately avoiding saying. Frequently this tactic is used when they are unsure how you will react. Are you really on their side? If you react badly they have the easy escape route of 'that's not what I meant'. Sadly, once they are sure of where you stand, even if this is in accord with their own view, they rarely bother to confirm this directly. This trick should not be confused with the legitimate use of tact and sensitivity. Nor in this case does it cover the desire to manipulate others using deliberate embellishments (watch the bookshops for *Spin Doctor* in the next instalment of Dirty Tricks at Work).

Indirectly Yours is often a cowardly game, which if they are honest with themselves, arises because they may not be able to handle an adverse reaction. So they dress up and confuse their messages to ensure that they feel safe. It is faulty thinking and frequently escalates and exacerbates the situation, as well as eroding the levels of trust that exist in relationships. Of course we need to be sensible about what we reveal about our own position. But at what point should we place our cards on the table? *Indirectly Yours* becomes a Dirty Trick when this point is exceeded unnecessarily and inappropriately for the circumstances.

From experience, we have seen many senior managers get so keen at using *Indirectly Yours* that everyone mistrusts their communication. The business risk of this habitual use was illustrated recently when a managing director, facing a serious threat to her business, gathered together the entire workforce. She wanted to inspire a great effort to head off the threat, to rally the troops. So she decided to be totally direct, for the first time ever. Unfortunately her employees, conditioned by years of oblique communications over-reacted and panic ensued because it was 'all over, we're finished'. The company went into meltdown.

GAME STATS: INDIRECTLY YOURS

PROFIT WARNING 4/10 (OVERALL, WHAT RISK DOES THIS PRESENT TO THE BOTTOM LINE FOR THE ORGANIZATION?)
Not a huge impact on the bottom line. The net effect of the confusion wrought with this trick is a reduction in management productivity and perhaps wasted resources when the work is not politically aligned. The most frequent casualties are presentations and reports, which need to be reworked several times until the positioning is correct.

ORG. SUSCEPTIBILITY 8/10 (HOW PRONE IS AN ORGANIZATION TO THIS TYPE OF BEHAVIOUR?)
The challenge with this trick is to know where to draw the line between sensible caution and deliberate manipulation. In any organization which has suffered several political casualties, people will become cautious. As fear grows, so does *Indirectly Yours*.

CULTURE THREAT 7/10 (HOW DOES THIS AFFECT THE ORGANIZATION CULTURE, AND STAFF MORALE?)
Indirectly Yours breeds confusion and distrust. If this sets in, the organization cannot even level with their staff without the messages being over-interpreted which as we saw earlier can have dramatic results.

PLAYER'S RISK RATING 5/10 (HOW RISKY IS IT FOR THE PLAYER TO PLAY THIS DIRTY TRICK AND RISK EXPOSURE?)
Players see this as a safe trick to play. Irrespective of the reaction they can explain themselves and feign both meanings. Yet they seem to be too short-sighted. The real risk they face is reduced trust and credibility. This is the long-term risk they run. It also suggests lack of confidence if they cannot directly state their views and thoughts.

VICTIM'S HEALTH WARNING 8/10 (WHAT RISK IS THE VICTIM PLACED UNDER WHEN THIS TRICK IS IN PLAY?)
How many times before you get that report right? The longer you suffer confusion and mixed messages the more it will impact your performance. You also run the risk that you will be perceived as naïve and politically inept. Not to mention that if you get suckered into disclosing your views, these could be used to your disadvantage on the political stage.

THE ANTIDOTE: INDIRECTLY YOURS

Because of the high personal risk and trouble it will cause you if you get caught by this Dirty Trick, we strongly recommend that in most cases this antidote is worth special attention.

To tackle this Dirty Trick, we first need to be able to identify when it is critical to know exactly what people are thinking or feeling. Then if we meet indirect comments, vague and indistinct remarks, we suggest that you gently, yet firmly, probe deeper using some or all of the smart questions below. Remember to be tactful because the person communicating with you in such an indirect manner may well feel that they are doing the right thing. They may also be afraid of revealing their true thoughts for some reason. Notice that some of these are not even questions in the technical sense, more conversation starters and probes designed to cut through the vagueness.

With these questions tone is vital. It is all too easy to ask these questions in a confrontational manner. Remember we want to understand and know what is really going on, not start a fight, so lightness and firm politeness are important!

POWER QUESTIONS TO ASK INDIRECTLY YOURS
- What do you really want to say?
- What are you feeling but not revealing?
- What message do you want me to take from that?
- What is really on your mind?
- I really want to know exactly what your thoughts are on this one ...
- That remark could be misinterpreted, please elaborate.
- What exactly did you mean when you said ...?
- I am not sure that I understand this correctly, can you explain what you mean another way please?
- Do you mean that ...?
- What stops you from telling me exactly what you really think?
- Please make explicit what you really mean ...
- There is a great danger of crossed wires here. Does this mean that ...?

If you feel the need to confront more directly and assertively (whilst at the same time keeping it light in tone) then it might sound something like this ...

'Surrinder, I am intrigued to know what you meant by describing you and Jerry as sparring partners?'
'Surrinder, I'm sorry but you are confusing me greatly. It is important that we are open and honest with each other and have clarity if we are to be successful. So

please tell me what you really think, as directly as you can. I promise to listen fairly to all you have to say and then give you an honest response.'

Before intervening remember that organizational conversation is riddled with indirect communication and you need to choose carefully when and how to intervene. Once you have made the choice to act, you need to decide how best to adapt this strategy to meet your specific needs. By giving it your best shot, you'll have signalled that you are politically astute and assertive. That you can cut through obtuse communication and you are not naïve. You will also have increased your chances of a successful outcome by acting assertively. Our experience is that you can't win them all, but with practice they'll soon learn they cannot get away with this trick.

THE POWER OF ...

DIRECTNESS
Organizational life is full of indirect communication. People very seldom say directly, cleanly and openly what they mean. Instead, many interactions are characterized by all manner of allusion and innuendo. This oblique conversational style provides Machiavelli with a cloak to hide under and conceal his tactics. The power of directness is that it is in such short supply. To choose to be direct, and at the same time polite and assertive, is to bring a refreshing candour to organizational conversation. Being a straight talker makes it easier for others to trust us because they know where we stand on a range of issues. We might not agree; however, others can be reassured by the openness and honesty of our opposition. Others seek us out for opinion and feedback because they are reassured that we will give them the clarity they need in a world full of conversational vagueness.

DIRTY TRICK NO. 8

JAM TOMORROW

Making vague promises of future rewards to encourage people to take on unpleasant assignments, put in more effort or take greater risks.

This game is all about encouraging someone to make sacrifices for implied (and frequently unnamed or unspecified) benefits to come later. This alleged 'promise' is presented in the secret knowledge that the real agenda is to manipulate them into taking on an assignment that they might reasonably say no to. It is a primitive motivation strategy, done in the belief that, given the rate of organizational change, it is unlikely that the promise will become due. Even if that day does arrive, the vagueness of the promise should allow the player to wriggle out easily.

In our mini drama we get just a taste of it when Surrinder, on her way out of the office at the end of her first meeting with Ben says: *'Ben ... who knows, you may even eclipse Jerry's star.'* You may also have noted that this was preceded with her desire to help him get the rewards he deserves. Go on, take a look again. No firm promise, no concrete commitment, just allusion to better things to come. Ben would be well advised to ask himself if Surrinder is realistically in any position to make such implied 'promises'.

Of course it is appropriate that we invest in our careers, and sometimes, with the long-term view in mind, it makes sense to take on assignments or projects we would rather not. The old adage 'you get out what you put in' is still a predominant outlook, and the reality is that most of us invest heavily in 'sacrificing' ourselves, in the hope of the next promotion. It is the meritocracy that exists in most organizations and it is a psychological contract that we understand.

Jam Tomorrow becomes a game when the reward is implied rather than stated directly and there is never any intention of delivering on the promise. This is a manipulative act and usually continues with new episodes until the victim gives up wanting the reward or believing that it will ever happen.

However, it is not just the usual Machiavellian types who resort to this tactic. Making vague promises about unsubstantiated possible future rewards is a common misguided management motivational technique, because what gets forgotten or ignored is the reality. The reality is that there are ever fewer senior positions and partnerships to be had, and any attempt to motivate the entire team under this 'promise' is a lie.

Managers interested in motivating team members in a more authentic fashion should do the work of finding out what each individual aspires to, wants and needs.

Then work creatively to make as much of that happen as possible. Playing *Jam Tomorrow* is a short-term strategy with a serious half-life for integrity.

GAME STATS: JAM TOMORROW

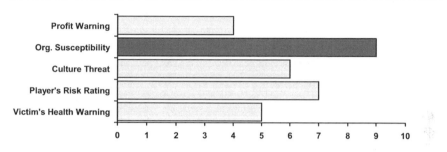

PROFIT WARNING 4/10 (OVERALL, WHAT RISK DOES THIS PRESENT TO THE BOTTOM LINE FOR THE ORGANIZATION?)
As with several other Dirty Tricks in this book, short-term there is not such a hit on the bottom line since the unwary victim will put in more effort than is perhaps justified, but watch the long-term motivation drop and progressive damage being done to the profitability of the business.

ORG. SUSCEPTIBILITY 9/10 (HOW PRONE IS AN ORGANIZATION TO THIS TYPE OF BEHAVIOUR?)
Is there anyone out there who hasn't been caught by this? With reducing opportunities for real promotion in flatter organizations the traditional motivational toolkit of managers is reducing rapidly. New ways exist but you can't 'teach an old dog new tricks'!

CULTURE THREAT 6/10 (HOW DOES THIS AFFECT THE ORGANIZATION CULTURE, AND STAFF MORALE?)
As this trick takes root in the organization trust diminishes quickly. Of particular note

with this trick is that the victims will readily talk about it when they realize they have been let down. There is also the tendency for suckers to get labelled and this opens the way for abuse by others as well.

PLAYER'S RISK RATING 7/10 (HOW RISKY IS IT FOR THE PLAYER TO PLAY THIS DIRTY TRICK AND RISK EXPOSURE?)
On the face of it this is not too risky; however, as time progresses the player will come under increasing pressure to deliver. This makes life awkward and the power balance starts to shift forcing the player to begin to make more and more excuses. At the same time a vital resource is becoming demotivated and probably spreading the bad feeling around to others.

VICTIM'S HEALTH WARNING 5/10 (WHAT RISK IS THE VICTIM PLACED UNDER WHEN THIS TRICK IS IN PLAY?)
At the end of the day you are going to be putting more effort in than is perhaps justified. However, treat it as an investment in your future. Just start to get realistic and become more adept at recognizing this manipulative act. The better you are able to distinguish the right things to do for your career the better.

THE ANTIDOTE: JAM TOMORROW

If you suspect that the jam you are being offered is little more than a manipulative act to get you to take on work you would otherwise run a mile from, then we prescribe the following interventions to check out the situation before you make your decision. Once again, the more smart questions you ask before you get out of the room or make your choice, the better informed you will be. Choose from the following list.

POWER QUESTIONS TO ASK BEFORE DECIDING
- You seem to be hinting at a reward to come later ... can you be more specific?
- Tell me more about the future rewards you are suggesting?
- How does this assignment prepare me for being a partner?
- Tell me more about ...
- What conversations have been had about me becoming a partner?
- It's a nice scenario, but what happens to your promise if you move on?
- What personal promise or commitment will you make to me at this stage?
- Who else has been lined up for the Florida assignment?
- Why have I been identified for this opportunity?
- What happens if I don't take the Luton assignment?
- How long does the Luton assignment last for?
- When do I need to make the decision?

The responses to these questions should not only help you in evaluating your choices, they should also clearly tell you, from the way the manager is responding, the extent to which they are being open and honest with you. Clearly if the manager is vague and non-committal, shifts uncomfortably in their chair and they appear defensive, then there is a very real chance that a game is in progress and they have been caught trying to manipulate you. If this is the case, it is time to get assertive and demonstrate some political savvy. You need to adapt this to meet your specific situation but for Ben, it might sound something like this ...

> 'Surrinder, I am here to do my best for Genesis so my motivation levels are high, but aside of your hints around Florida, I am curious to know what rewards you are prepared to commit to now.'

Or, back in Chapter One, before agreeing to move to Luton and take on Genesis, Ben could have challenged Jerry with ...

'Jerry, I am just not convinced. One of the oldest games in town is to get someone to take on new work by making vague promises about their future career. Now, I want us to be more open and honest with each other. Let's put our cards on the table and have the real conversation and get away from these hints and vague promises.'

Go on, look back at Chapter One. Chances are you missed it amongst the many other lines that Jerry was fishing with to motivate poor Ben. This is an all too common tactic because one of the hooks will surely land a fish. This direct approach has the advantage of inviting the manager into an honest conversation and suggests to them very clearly that you are not about to be manipulated. Despite the gamey strategy they are indulging in, you can still be professional about this.

The next step is for you to decide how best to adapt these ideas to suit your situation. Sadly there is never one right way or a guaranteed strategy; however, we believe that if you intervene assertively and professionally using these ideas as a guide then you will have taken a significant step towards getting a successful outcome.

The bottom line is that you will have demonstrated your self-confidence and political savvy and provided that you do this assertively, then you will have signalled that you are nobody's fool. Better, when done correctly, you should emerge from this situation with your personal power enhanced and your credibility and integrity intact!

THE POWER OF ...

DOING NOTHING

A paradoxical idea perhaps, given that all our strategies are about assertive action, but this is definitely one worth considering. Doing nothing (at least initially) gives us a chance to think and put aside the anger, hurt and frustration we feel in the moment. Doing nothing gives us the chance to compose ourselves and get our thinking switched on and emotions under control. Even more bizarre is that sometimes doing nothing and ignoring a Machiavellian ploy is the best thing we can do, especially if we suspect that the Machiavellian game is one which was simply designed just to invite us into feeling bad. Doing nothing avoids the 'uproar' that Machiavelli was probably trying to prompt and rewards you with the moral high ground. Knowing when to act and when to do nothing is a powerful political skill.

DIRTY TRICK NO. 9

GUARDIAN ANGEL

The tactic of implying friendly support, whilst at the same time suggesting that there are other more powerful people to answer to, who will be much tougher, unless co-operation is quickly forthcoming.

Guardian Angel is the game of taking a position of implied empathy to 'protect' another person from the unseen enemy. The enemy, usually a more powerful and challenging person, is never in the room at the time. Moreover, this enemy may well take over the situation, unless a better agreement is quickly, and willingly forthcoming. A variant on this trick is *Good Cop*, where the enemy – the bad cop – is always present. Unfortunately we don't have space to elaborate on this, but watch out for the next book.

The apparent game positions[2] are that the *Guardian Angel* takes the role of rescuer to the victim, and suggests that the persecutor (the enemy) is just the other side of the door waiting to get at them. However the reality is that the *Guardian Angel* is really the persecutor in disguise, attempting to elicit co-operation disingenuously. Enemies may be invented or, unfortunately, be all-too-real characters whose reputation precedes them.

In reality, this Dirty Trick comes from a whole family of tactics favoured by Machiavellian types in the workplace. There are times when this Dirty Trick even skirts around the edge of becoming bullying which adds a more sinister angle to this game which, despite the severity, is not really the subject of this book. In our modest mini drama we notice Surrinder playing *Guardian Angel* as she attempts to coerce and manipulate Ben about his strategy and plans for Genesis.

> 'Believe me Ben, dealing with me will be much easier than having to present to the MD directly. If you think Jerry is an ogre, wait until you have dealt with the big boss himself.'

We notice how Jerry and the MD are positioned as enemies and Surrinder attempts to position herself as coming to Ben's rescue. The reality of course is that Surrinder simply doesn't like Ben's strategy and is attempting to manipulate him into changing it to meet her needs and criteria. Whenever we are pressured by someone claiming that there are absent, powerful others who will be unpleasant or difficult about what we are proposing, then the likelihood is that *Guardian Angel* is in play.

---

[2] To find out more about Steve Karpman's game positions, google on 'drama triangles' 'karpman'.

GAME STATS: GUARDIAN ANGEL

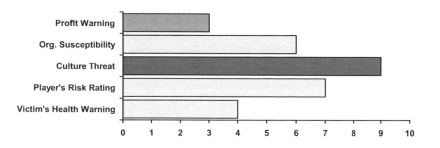

PROFIT WARNING 3/10 (OVERALL, WHAT RISK DOES THIS PRESENT TO THE BOTTOM LINE FOR THE ORGANIZATION?)
This is another trick that doesn't cause immediate damage to the bottom line. But as the culture changes customers and employees will start to avoid your company in ever increasing numbers. You cannot keep talented staff with threats, and these are the very people who can ensure your long-term profitability.

ORG. SUSCEPTIBILITY 6/10 (HOW PRONE IS AN ORGANIZATION TO THIS TYPE OF BEHAVIOUR?)
As it becomes more and more difficult to motivate people using traditional techniques, the temptation becomes strong to resort to this tactic. Even more likely to happen if there really are fearsome ogres in high places.

CULTURE THREAT 9/10 (HOW DOES THIS AFFECT THE ORGANIZATION CULTURE, AND STAFF MORALE?)
This breeds a climate of fear. Perhaps tolerable in strong command and control cultures but in the modern business world is this really what will maximize the motivation of the workforce? We think not.

PLAYER'S RISK RATING 7/10 (HOW RISKY IS IT FOR THE PLAYER TO PLAY THIS DIRTY TRICK AND RISK EXPOSURE?)
The bottom line is that if you resort to this trick and are exposed, it will hit your credibility hard. If this is all you've got left in your toolbox to gain co-operation, the overriding impression will be that you're on your way out. Knowledge and confidence is required to motivate people authentically and most victims will notice your deficiency quickly.

VICTIM'S HEALTH WARNING 4/10 (WHAT RISK IS THE VICTIM PLACED UNDER WHEN THIS TRICK IS IN PLAY?)
What is it actually going to cost you to comply? If it is a reasonable request from a weak player you'll probably just be left with a bad taste in your mouth. Once you are aware of this trick, steps can be taken to minimize the damage safely even in the most severe cases.

THE ANTIDOTE: GUARDIAN ANGEL

Other writers and sales trainers have suggested to us that the most effective way to confront this game is to match *Guardian Angel* with your own version of the trick. In other words, when they attempt to manipulate you by raising the difficulty they will have with their boss, you come right back at them by suggesting that you too have an ogre back in the office to report to.

We accept that whilst this tactic can and does work, it does little to increase the levels of trust and honesty in the relationship. As the players confront each other the situation can quickly escalate. After all, 'my dad's bigger than yours' is another game that we all learn in the playground and have probably modified (only slightly) for use in the office. Once a stalemate occurs, players will try to fall back on other Dirty Tricks as they attempt a WIN/LOSE[3] outcome. If we are to be successful then we need to put

---

[3] If you are not familiar with WIN/LOSE, WIN/WIN we suggest you check out Stephen Covey's *Seven Habits of Highly Effective People*, published by Simon & Schuster.

aside our desire to be manipulative and coercive and look for more authentic ways of resolving the impasse.

To move the negotiation on to a more productive level the positive politician will use their skills to find a way to make explicit, the implicit ulterior motives. To expose a game is to reduce its potency and provided we do this in a way that quickly invites constructive ideas for moving things forward, it can increase personal credibility, power and integrity. In the context of our story, Ben might have said something more constructive like this ...

> 'Surrinder, thanks for your concern but I am relatively unfazed at dealing with Jerry or the old man. I wonder what is really behind your concern because it seems that what I am proposing doesn't meet your needs. Let's talk though how this deal could work for you.'

or ...

> 'Surrinder, I am interested in making sure that all stakeholders can buy into this strategy for Genesis, so I'd like to know more about your concerns and how you perceive the positions that Jerry and the old man are likely to take.'

An alternative, but higher risk/reward method for derailing this trick is to call their bluff, but you may need a strong position and stomach. For example:

> 'Surrinder, I appreciate your concern and I'd like to settle this uncertainty now. Let's get Jerry on the phone and discuss it directly with him, or perhaps we can have a frank discussion about the concerns you would have taking this to him.'

At the very least you'll get a much more direct and honest communication with the implied threat removed. The player will also be more careful next time! Research continues to demonstrate that most people learn political savvy using trial and error. This takes time as one of our clients recently recounted how he learned to deal with *Guardian Angel.*

'As a young manager, I was once warned that my "highly creative" ideas around re-merchandising a famous retail store would never be entertained by the ferocious director, and that a "blander" plan would be in everyone's best interests, especially the store manager. However, undeterred, when I next saw the allegedly "ferocious director" in store I brazenly made my suggestion, which was immediately accepted as a great idea. The director, who in actual fact was pretty ferocious, immediately instructed my manager to implement my ideas. I resisted the urge for further mischief here by dropping the manager in it. The happy ending came six months later when the director and my manager both put me forward for promotion to the Head Office team. I also now realize the risk I ran with the manager, but hey, I was a rookie okay.'

THE POWER OF ...

THE BANK OF INTEGRITY

If you have decided to take positive action, then check in with yourself about your own personal values first. It is important to ensure that whatever strategy you choose does not damage your integrity, self-esteem and self-worth. For a Machiavellian type there is little or no conflict here, they believe that the end always justifies the means, however high the body count gets. But for most of us, when we act in manipulative ways we can easily undermine our personal values. This emotional dissonance (the gap between our values and our actions) causes stress and damages our self-esteem and integrity. An overdraft at the Bank of Integrity has punitive interest rates so we must ensure that we always stay 'in the black' and avoid making withdrawals. Acting with integrity, reducing the amount of manipulation we engage in and acting authentically all serve to build up healthy reserves and earn good interest.

CHAPTER FOUR

ESCALATION AND ATTRITION

It took Ben the rest of the morning to calm down following his disappointing encounter with Patak. Sitting at his desk he tried to make sense of it all but couldn't. Once again, his naïve desire to just concentrate on doing a good job, without considering the politics around it, had sabotaged his plans. Ben wondered, with negative politics apparently being so rife across the organization, how anything ever got done.

His laptop let out that gentle, yet distracting 'ping' that signalled incoming mail. He checked his inbox.

From: Jerry Ottaker
To: Senior Management Action Committee
Cc: Ann Summer
Subject: Strategic Away Day
Attachments: lygonmap.pdf (28kb)
Given the sorry state of project Genesis and the lack of urgency being demonstrated by some Xennic outstations, I have decided to bring forward the next SAD. The revised dates will now be from 18.00 on the 26 November through to 12.00 on the 28 November. Everyone in the SMAC will be required to present a detailed

account of their plans to me, for sign off and approval, and it goes without saying that this must include proposals on how you intend to support Genesis going forward.

I am sure that I do not need to stress the importance of your personal attention and attendance at this business critical meeting. Please return your confirmations to Ann Summer in Admin Support ASAP.

Jerry.

Ben did not need to look at his calendar to know that these revised dates would now be over a weekend. Another threat to his work–life balance. Along with more depression, this also added to his stress levels because he now had even less time to pull his plan together. At this stage he couldn't even get it approved by Patak, so what chance did he have of getting SMAC sign off? A short while later another message arrived in his inbox.

From: Surrinder Patak
To: Jerry Ottaker
Cc: Senior Management Action Committee; Ann Summer; Directors
Subject: Strategic Away Day
Attachments: SAD Objectives.doc (36kb)
Dearest Jerry,
With reference to your earlier message, please find attached the objectives agreed at the last SAD; now updated with notes about how the Luton team have met nearly all objectives within agreed timescales. I am very much looking forward to reading about any progress the London team have might have made, but nevertheless have realistic expectations about this.
With Kindest and Warmest Regards
Surrinder.

Ben's immediate thought was of admiration from Surrinder. She was certainly flying the flag for Luton and was letting Jerry know that she was getting on with things, even if she was coming on a bit strong in the last sentence. He reflected back on his conversation with Russell Bromley-Clarke that Surrinder and Jerry were 'mortal enemies', and this bore that theory out. He was speculating about the intensity of this dislike and how on earth he was ever going to come up with a project plan for Genesis that would keep everyone happy, when his laptop 'pinged' again.

From: Jerry Ottaker
To: Surrinder Patak
Cc: Directors; Senior Management Action Committee, Jim Bloomberg
Subject: Strategic Away Day
Attachments:
Thank you for the reminder Surrinder. As always, all SMAC members will be required to present their progress against objectives at the SAD, which is in line with our usual process. Sadly I still seem to need to remind some outstations that London now only carries the executive responsibility for Genesis and that any actions pertaining to London, agreed at the last SAD have, along with Ben Waterstone, now been transferred to the Luton office. I therefore still expect to know what progress has been made by the Luton contingent, now that they have been in a position to optimize the additional resource that I generously made available. It is frustrating that I still need to remind some of you where your responsibilities lie.
Jerry.

Another 'ping'.

From: Surrinder Patak
To: Jerry Ottaker
Bcc: Ben Waterstone
Subject: Strategic Away Day
Attachments: GenesisNew.doc (104kb)

Dearest Jerry,
Please find attached a message from Sir William Henry Smith (Group CEO) outlining his ideas for where he believes responsibility for sign off with Genesis should reside. You will notice that he is clear that executive authority should reside within his domain and that he is looking to the Luton office to be the main mover and shaker in this process. Whilst London may be the capital city, as far as Genesis is concerned it would seem that Luton is currently of greater strategic importance. I do however thank you for your increasing concerns over Genesis and look forward to hearing about your progress against outstanding action points, as we discussed earlier.
With Warmest Regards
Surrinder

Ben was puzzled. It was unclear exactly what they were arguing about but he needed to find a way to unravel it if he was going to survive Genesis. Ben also noticed that this rather public squabble had now been restricted to just the three of them. Ben wondered if Jerry knew about the Bcc function, but given that Lewis was his henchman, he suspected that he knew this little tactic.

From: Jerry Ottaker
To: Surrinder Patak
Cc:
Subject: Private and Confidential
Attachments:
Having discussed Genesis at some length with Sir Bill over the weekend at the golf tournament I am reassured that he and I are still in agreement that London will retain executive authority for Genesis. Sir Bill and I go back a long way and I know him well enough to know that he would never sanction the transference of key business authorities from London to Luton. It is such a shame that you do not play golf; otherwise you might not be so handicapped!
J.

Ben was not immediately privy to the above message that Jerry had sent, however, Surrinder was kind enough to forward a copy to him with the question 'Now do you see what we have to deal with?' Then came her final salvo.

> From: Surrinder Patak
> To: Jerry Ottaker
> Bcc: Ben Waterstone
> Subject: Private and Confidential
> Dearest Jerry,
> I think that it is important for all of us to remember how we got into this mess, and I think certain people need to take responsibility for their actions. Last night I was reminded of this when perusing my photos of last year's Christmas Ball. I assume you'll be along again to enjoy yourself, and I know that Ann Summers will be attending again. Such a nice picture. By the way, will Mrs Ottaker be coming along to join in the fun this year?
> Anyway, I am looking forward to your co-operation at the meeting, and in future please be kind enough to consult me whenever changing SAD dates.
> As always, assuring you of my closest of attentions and with warmest regards
> Surrinder.

Ben reeled at the sheer nerve of it all. Surrinder could play hardball all right and Bromley-Clark was dead right about the special relationship between Jerry and Surrinder. But how the hell was he going to navigate a safe course for Genesis while this power struggle raged?

CHAPTER FOUR: MENTORING INTERVENTION

In the several thousand years of organizational history, e-mail has been with us for a very short time indeed, yet it is fascinating to recognize the extent to which it has become such a key business communication tool. Ironically it also has to be acknowledged that whilst this clearly means more communication between people, it is highly questionable if this has led to better communication. Indeed the more we ask around, the more that everyone has a tale to tell about how e-mail has been used aggressively or disingenuously against them.

Given that the psychological root of political games can usually be traced back to low self-confidence and self-esteem, lack of assertion and inappropriate uses of power (alongside good old myopic self-interest) it is hardly surprising that political games have been able to flourish in cyberspace, hence the reason for Chapter Four being mostly emails.

And so we see Ben witness to a spat between the two 'arch enemies'. Waging war in cyberspace. Not particularly pleasant, nor uncommon within large organizations the world over. Before we explore the Dirty Tricks evident in this chapter, ask yourself the following questions:

- Reading between the lines, what do you think is really going on here?
- What impact does this have on the key players' credibility amongst the witnesses?
- What conclusions can you draw from this episode?
- Is Luton really this well connected to the information superhighway?
- Have you been witness to this sort of exchange of fire?
- Have you ever engaged? What happened?
- If you were Surrinder, what would you have done differently?
- What should Ben do now?
- Have you ever misbehaved at a Christmas party? (don't answer!)

We want you to be honest with yourself here. As you read the next page, ask yourself to what extent have you played these Dirty Tricks? Easily done, but do you know where to draw the line? If you are guilty, we won't tell anyone but seriously consider what impact this could have on your personal credibility and also your effectiveness.

Let's move on with the mayhem ...

THE DIRTY TRICKS IN CHAPTER FOUR

DIRTY TRICK NO. 10: E-MAIL TO THE GODS
Using e-mail to shame or coerce another. Usually an e-mail arriving from a colleague (which includes either true or false information) levelling accusations of blame, which are also copied on to bosses, directors, customers, suppliers etc.

DIRTY TRICK NO. 11: NAME DROPPER
The tactic of coercing another by suggesting that friends in high places are supporters/detractors and will be drafted unless agreement is quickly forthcoming.

DIRTY TRICK NO. 12: EXPOSURE
Coercing others by threatening to make public their professional/personal failings or secret and sensitive information.

DIRTY TRICK NO. 10

E-MAIL TO THE GODS

Using e-mail to shame or coerce another. This is usually an e-mail arriving from a colleague (which includes either true or false information) levelling accusations of blame, which are also copied on to bosses, directors, customers, suppliers etc.

E-mail to the Gods was the first political game in cyberspace that we were able to isolate and describe succinctly enough to be able to prescribe a suitable antidote. We define it as using e-mail to publicly shame or coerce another. It usually takes the form of an e-mail arriving from a colleague, levelling accusations of blame, but which is also copied on to bosses, directors, customers or even suppliers, so that powerful others in the organization are informed about the incompetence of another. It is of course appropriate to Cc important people for e-mails that directly concern them; however, that is clearly not the intent here.

The evidence of this trick creates a clear audit trail as soon as they are sent. They can be stored indefinitely to be used in evidence at a later date and can be easily screened by security or IT departments. You would think that this awareness would discourage it.

Those who are politically astute know this and take great care to ensure that their messages and responses cannot be used against them, but it is surprising just how many still get this wrong, or fail to intervene effectively if they are caught up in a political e-mail game. Many surveys have confirmed that people are more aggressive with their message style and content when communicating over e-mail (or letter) than they would ever be face-to-face. It is likely you have had the experience of challenging someone over the tough or formal tone of a communication they have sent only to get a reply along the lines of 'sorry about that, I had to use official language, let me explain ...'

Because e-mail fails to carry the emotional data supporting the message, it is frequently misinterpreted and responded to ineffectively. Players who are careless, politically naïve, or whose emotional intelligence has temporarily deserted them, dash off accusations and insults over e-mail without thinking more deeply or strategically.

People who have told us their experiences of this game also recognize that it seems to matter little if the accusation is true or false, or if elements are exaggerated, because the intent seems to be more about undermining another than solving the problem. The persecutors who indulge in this tactic also know that once an accusation is out there, regardless of its accuracy or truth, and regardless of any public exoneration that might follow, that some of the mud sticks and that reputations can be undermined in this way. In the public domain there are a lot of very rich libel lawyers!

Another unpleasant aspect of this game is the way in which the opening moves invite other bystanders to join in the game, thereby escalating the mayhem and encouraging more manipulative and political acts as line managers and directors take sides and dictate their own version of events. None of this has anything to do with getting on and doing good work, it is just unhelpful politicking. It needs cutting through if we are to get on and leverage business performance.

The stories that people tell us tend to suggest that the initial move by the persecutor who starts this game, seems to be motivated by blaming and shaming another, and that the response from the victim can often be about counter accusations and blame shifting; however, it seems that it can also equally be about inviting a rescue from these other more powerful bystanders. Non-assertive people can use *E-mail to the Gods* as a cry for help, and this only exacerbates the problem.

A variation of this game that we have also identified is where the Bcc function is used[1]. The fun part is that if the receiver of the message simply hits 'Reply to All' when responding, all the previously hidden e-mail names and addresses are then revealed, along with the duplicity of the game! This unexpected feature is in at least one of the largest e-mail programs used by many large corporations. Be warned.

E-mail to the Gods is endemic in organizations and this huge waste of time and energy needs to be tackled.

---

[1] Just in case, Bcc means 'blind carbon copy', and enables you to copy in other people without the receiver of the message being aware that you have done so.

GAME STATS: E-MAIL TO THE GODS

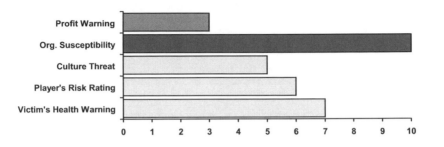

PROFIT WARNING 3/10 (OVERALL, WHAT RISK DOES THIS PRESENT TO THE BOTTOM LINE FOR THE ORGANIZATION?)
The impact here is on your server space and bandwidth getting clogged up with unnecessary e-mails and attachments. And we wonder why IT departments all over the world keep threatening to delete unless we clear up our inboxes. You also have to be mindful of the negative impact of all the time that this trick consumes. What else could everyone be doing to improve the bottom line?

ORG. SUSCEPTIBILITY 10/10 (HOW PRONE IS AN ORGANIZATION TO THIS TYPE OF BEHAVIOUR?)
The pressure is on to get results. The temptation to rush off an e-mail to try to manipulate others is great. Is there anyone out there who has not been on the receiving end of this one? Is there anyone out there who has not responded?

CULTURE THREAT 5/10 (HOW DOES THIS AFFECT THE ORGANIZATION CULTURE, AND STAFF MORALE?)
The use of this trick is not a particularly serious threat to the culture unless it becomes vicious and the usual reaction of recipients is to join in. However, e-mail overuse is endangering healthy communication within organizations.

PLAYER'S RISK RATING 6/10 (HOW RISKY IS IT FOR THE PLAYER TO PLAY THIS DIRTY TRICK AND RISK EXPOSURE?)
Who do you think you are kidding? Exposure is guaranteed because you've done it yourself. As soon as this book becomes a best-seller people will quickly see what you are doing and their respect for you will drop like a lead balloon.

VICTIM'S HEALTH WARNING 7/10 (WHAT RISK IS THE VICTIM PLACED UNDER WHEN THIS TRICK IS IN PLAY?)
It hurts when you are accused so publicly in this way. The amount of time you then have to spend considering the carefully worded reply will pull you away from other pressing work on your schedule. If you take the bait, multiply the victim score by the player risk score and you'll see you're onto a loser!

THE ANTIDOTE: E-MAIL TO THE GODS

This game can be tackled using e-mail, but we strongly suggest that if at all possible you deal with it face-to-face, or at least over the phone. *E-mail to the Gods* is an aggressive strategy for influencing, and the power of the face-to-face meeting lies in the fact that whoever is playing this game, was probably gambling on you retaliating or capitulating using the same communication channel. They are probably hoping that you will weaken your position by starting an 'e-mail fight' which they can then use to complain further about you. Remember, e-mail leaves a clear trail, which can be used in evidence against you.

Look back at the chapter. You will see that the distribution list grows a little with each exchange until the players take the gloves off. This is being done in an attempt to add further embarrassment and is a call to supporters to take note and potentially join their side.

On a recent workshop one delegate recognized that she was caught up in playing this game and that it was sapping her energy and morale as well as ruining her concentration. At the next break she made a quick call to her persecutor, who was surprised and taken aback by her directness and confidence, and she agreed a better way forward with him. When she returned to the group she was noticeably more relaxed and proud of her ability to take assertive action. Suffice to say we were all impressed.

Meeting face-to-face (or talking on the phone) demonstrates your self-confidence and personal power (even if you don't feel it) as well as your willingness to sort the issue out professionally. This gives you the moral high ground and, provided you can be assertive (i.e. defend your position without infringing their rights), you will dramatically increase your chances of success. We also suggest that you meet them on their 'home ground' and consider also not making an appointment. That way you signal to them your confidence and desire to act quickly and decisively and because of the element of surprise, they will be less likely to have developed an alternative version of events, or found new games to use as a cover-up.

Another lady reported back to us that when she was on the receiving end of a particularly scathing *E-mail to the Gods* from a director, she just popped round the corner to his office and sat on his desk. 'He was scared to death, caught like a rabbit in the headlights. The matter ended there with profuse apologies.' We think he'll be more careful next time!

As you prepare, notice how you are feeling about this situation and make a commitment to yourself that whatever happens, you will stay calm, focused and not allow your emotions to cloud your message. Remember, the last thing you need will be a stand-up row, which risks escalation and attrition and reduces your chances of success. Remember also that if they get angry, throw a tantrum, shout, point, swear and scream, but you are able to stay calm and focused, whatever else happens, you will emerge with your integrity and self-esteem intact.

Before you set up the meeting get your facts and your story straight. Read the e-mail audit trail and notice the key elements of the disagreement and prepare accordingly. Spend some time actually writing down the key messages you need to say; that way you will get greater clarity. Use the power questions that appear below as a framework, to further increase your chances of a good meeting.

When you have got the message composed, find a trusted friend and a quiet corner and rehearse it out loud – yes, really! This is not role-play, but rehearsal for a real-life, high-stakes situation that needs all of your skills and preparation. Tell the friend before you start that you want to hear their feedback, so prepare them by asking them to notice how clear the message is, and what they experience as you delivered it. Remember, you need to come across as assertive rather than aggressive. Value their feedback, act on it, and thank them. Now go and meet the gamey person who thinks that shaming people by e-mail is an effective way to manage effective working relationships!

POWER QUESTIONS TO ASK IN THE MEETING
- What was on your mind when you sent this e-mail?
- In what ways has the situation changed since your e-mail?
- What were you hoping to achieve by copying in my boss, your boss etc.?
- What impact do you think it might have had on those you copied in?
- What impact did you intend this e-mail to have on me?
- How are you feeling about the situation now?
- What would be an ideal outcome from this situation for you now?
- What should we both do in future to avoid this happening again?

The good news is that if you are bold enough to face up to this trick appropriately, then people will start to recognize your political skills and they will quickly learn that they need to think very carefully before they try *E-mail to the Gods* again. Once you've handled it a few times, your confidence will grow and this problem can almost disappear so you can get on with more important work.

THE POWER OF ...

REHEARSAL
Behind every brilliant performance a huge amount of rehearsal took place. Elite sports performers, stars of stage and screen and yes, even politicians, understand the power and importance of rehearsal. Alistair Campbell spent hours

coaching and rehearsing Tony Blair through all the keynote speeches in advance. A great number of famous people have been credited with the quote 'the harder I practise, the luckier I get'. Perfect performance is not luck, it is the apparently effortless execution of skill that has been practised and rehearsed to perfection. Expecting to be successful in an interaction with Machiavelli when just going in and 'winging it' might work, but it also dramatically increases the chances that something will go wrong. Rehearsal, preferably with a trusted friend or adviser who is well placed to give you constructive feedback and coaching, restores the balance and is much more likely to lead to a powerful performance.

NAME DROPPER

The tactic of coercing another by suggesting that friends in high places are supporters/detractors and will be drafted in unless agreement is quickly forthcoming.

Name Dropper is one of the clearest examples of games that we learn in early childhood and rehearse and refine as we move from playground to boardroom. As children we quickly realize that in situations where our own personal power is insufficient to influence events, that invoking the power of an absent another can often be potent. 'My dad says ...' or 'Mrs Reed told me to tell you to ...'

As we refine and rehearse *Name Dropper* as a child, we also discover that it matters little if the person whose name we are dropping has actually authorized us so, or is even aware that we are using their tacit power. We discover that we can move from invoking the power of another, into creating power for ourselves by exploiting absent others. We learn fast and discover that this is a tempting strategy to use as our awareness of covert power and influence grows. So, in the playground it is legitimate to pass on the message that Mrs Reed has sent; however, if there never was a conversation with Mrs Reed or a message to pass on, and we are appropriating her power in her absence to influence events, then we have learned one of our first political games.

And so it continues on into organizational life. Whenever an individual encounters a situation where they believe that their own personal power will be insufficient to get things done, then the power of others can be invoked. This can be legitimate and not a political game. In our mini melodrama in Chapter Four, Jerry is trying to coerce Surrinder by *Name Dropping* about his relationship with the MD. Notice how Sir William Henry Smith the CEO is casually abbreviated to simply Sir Bill to reinforce the suggestion of a strong bond.

For another example: if the MD asks a manager to do something on their behalf and whilst doing so, their authority is questioned, it would be appropriate to let others know that they are acting under the mandate of the MD. Similarly if they play golf with the MD regularly or know them socially and they are asked directly if they know the MD personally, it is honest of them to disclose this information.

However *Name Dropper* becomes a Dirty Trick when the relationship that is referred to is either exaggerated, non-existent, or has been invoked as a means of wielding inappropriate personal power. The *Name Dropper* often wants to fool people into thinking that there are powerful people who have already been consulted, that are on their side, in the hope that they will realize the forces aligned against them will make success unlikely.

Imagine you are on your way to the boardroom to make a key presentation. As you move towards the boardroom doors you are intercepted by a persecutor who casually opines ...

> 'Good luck with your presentation to the board. By the way, I was with Jerry and Sir Bill over the weekend (we've been friends a long while now and we were having a barbeque to celebrate our daughters A level results); anyhow, they mentioned your idea ... yeah we all had a good laugh about it. It's a shame that they are in such a foul mood today. Anyhow, good luck!'

This is using *Name Dropper* to deliberately undermine our self-confidence and concentration. It is a naked power play. Even if events at the barbeque were as described, and the relationships are as suggested, there is clearly a Machiavellian tactic at work here.

GAME STATS: NAME DROPPER

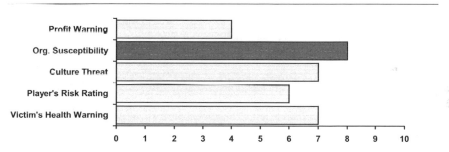

PROFIT WARNING 4/10 (OVERALL, WHAT RISK DOES THIS PRESENT TO THE BOTTOM LINE FOR THE ORGANIZATION?)
Much depends on the players' motives. If they are acting out of self-interest, beware of

the impact on profits. Generally this trick is used to tip the balance in the influencing game, to nudge someone an extra inch towards compliance. Because of this, the victim probably has good reasons for resisting, hopefully for the good of the organization.

ORG. SUSCEPTIBILITY 8/10 (HOW PRONE IS AN ORGANIZATION TO THIS TYPE OF BEHAVIOUR?)
With demand for ever-precious resources from conflicting projects, it is very tempting for individuals to *Name Drop* as they compete. It's such an easy trick to play, sometimes even unwittingly.

CULTURE THREAT 7/10 (HOW DOES THIS AFFECT THE ORGANIZATION CULTURE, AND STAFF MORALE?)
With people having to resort to such lies, the culture is quickly going to get bogged down. How healthy is it to have a culture that replies on deceit to move things forward?

PLAYER'S RISK RATING 6/10 (HOW RISKY IS IT FOR THE PLAYER TO PLAY THIS DIRTY TRICK AND RISK EXPOSURE?)
Since you are misrepresenting your relationship with a powerful individual, how will they view this if it comes to their attention? Because you are using their name inappropriately, they may be quite upset and you'll have to explain yourself. Excessive use also damages personal credibility and displays a lack of clear thinking and logic, not to mention confidence.

VICTIM'S HEALTH WARNING 7/10 (WHAT RISK IS THE VICTIM PLACED UNDER WHEN THIS TRICK IS IN PLAY?)
A great deal depends on how you react and the impact on your work if you comply. If you get suckered in on this one it will happen again, and again. At the end of the day, you are losing control of what you do and your best-laid plans for performing will get derailed.

THE ANTIDOTE: NAME DROPPER

Firstly remember that *Name Dropper* is extremely common in organizational interactions and that many names are 'dropped'. If legitimate requests positioned in a non-assertive manner are accompanied by a 'name'; we should co-operate if it is appropriate to do so. This antidote deals with those times when our internal radar warns us that all is not right with this conversation, and that the opening moves of a game are in play.

As we identified earlier, *Name Dropper* is a game that most of us encounter and learn at a young age as we move from playground to boardroom. Because it has been a part of our human interactions for a long time, it has embedded itself deeply into our personal programming. This is significant because now, as a fully joined-up member of the adult community, when we encounter someone using *Name Dropper* against us we react automatically. Our deep programming is likely to kick in and we may well respond with emotions and attitudes that were connected to our earlier experiences, hence we may well react or respond inappropriately.

The first step towards dealing with a *Name Dropper* is to notice our immediate emotional reaction quickly, and assess its relative usefulness in this situation. If we notice that we want to react as a seven-year-old, then perhaps this is not the most integrity building strategy to use. The second, and more useful strategy, might well be to 'do nothing'. Remember the encounter with our adversary on our way to the boardroom? If you are confident that the *Name Dropper* is simply using this to undermine your concentration or confidence and it is a power play, then ignoring it is both effective and appropriate.

Remember, the intent behind this version of the game is about power and interfering with your performance. Any reaction on our part hands the persecutor the victory they crave. The key, as we stride confidently into the boardroom, is to run more helpful mental software where we self-coach ourselves into concentrating on delivering an excellent presentation.

The third useful strategy, especially if simply ignoring the persecutor is not an option, is to ask smart questions. Persecutors who instigate games are usually expecting a fight or flight response from us, so to stay calm and ask good questions from an adult and assertive standpoint is not what they expect. Furthermore, remember that the last thing a game player wants is to be exposed and this strategy enables you to remain polite and responsive.

POWER QUESTIONS TO ASK THE NAME DROPPER
If Lewis says … 'the MD, Jim – or JB to his friends – suggested to me over the weekend that I am next in line for the Florida assignment', consider challenging him with the following, using a friendly, enquiring tone:

- What's going on, Lewis?
- What did the MD actually say? (Note: if you get a vague or indefinite answer to this question then it is almost certainly a game!)
- What is the connection between you and the MD?
- How well do you know the MD?
- How would the MD feel if he knew you were discussing this with me?
- What reaction would I get if I asked him directly to clarify the position?
- What are you hoping to achieve by telling me this?
- Who else is in line for Florida?
- What reason would the MD have for being so indiscreet?
- What else did the MD say?

More importantly, by asking questions you demonstrated that you are not going to be intimidated. You are politically savvy, have high levels of emotional intelligence and you are confident and mature. In other words, a persecutor's nightmare!

The more direct delegates we have worked with favour a final strategy. Their preference is for highlighting the game and then offering the chance for more authentic ways forward that might work for both of you. In this context it might sound something like this …

'Lewis, is this a game where you keep dropping the names of all the senior partners in the hope of giving me a message? I want us to be more authentic than this, so how about you tell me what is really on your mind?'

And, depending on your relationship with Lewis and your interpersonal style, you might like to get especially direct and give them the message that you are not to be fooled with.

> 'Lewis, I know you don't know the MD as well as you are suggesting, so what are you trying to say here? Let's get on and have the real conversation we both need, eh?'

Alternatively, you could of course make the suggestion of calling the powerful other for clarification. Then watch the player wriggle out of that one!

THE POWER OF ...

WHAT AND WHO
What you know will always be a vital commodity in your career. And you will almost certainly have learned that who you know is also just as important. Not more important, but as important. Getting the balance right between what you know and who you know is important. Spend too long just working on the 'who' part detracts from our core purpose. But what towers above the both of these is our ability to influence others when we interact with them. It is all very well 'collecting' people, building positive relationships, networking and staying in the loop, but there is little point if, in our interactions with others, we do not maximize our impact and effectiveness. Core-influencing skills can be learned, so explore the huge range of training options out there so that we can ensure that in every interpersonal interaction we make a good impression and add useful people into our network.

DIRTY TRICK NO. 12

EXPOSURE

Coercing others by threatening to make public their professional/personal failings or secret and sensitive information.

As with *Name Dropper*, *Exposure* is learned at a young age and rehearsed and refined as we grow up. It has its roots in 'telling tales' when as children we discover that we can successfully coerce others by using this tactic. We also discover that when we carry out our threat, we often get grown-up approval for acting in this way. This reinforces our belief that this is a good way to get our needs met. Our pay-off is not only grown-up approval, but also a triumph over those we would persecute. This double pay-off is potently reinforcing, so no wonder we rehearse and refine it for later use.

Of course it is sometimes appropriate to give people information we have discovered that is important for the greater good of all, or that we are contracted or obliged to disclose. If a child exposes a fellow pupil's penchant for breaking windows at school then, provided the motive for exposure is to protect the school and the health and safety of others, then this is appropriate and not a game. However, if having discovered this information it is withheld and only communicated to the window-breaker to coerce or elicit a reward (sweets perhaps), then a game has begun and a Dirty Trick is being practised.

Where our early programming can get confused is when we act with positive intent, only to be rounded on by parents, teachers and others as 'snitches' or worse. This confusion places doubt in our minds about using *Exposure* as a game and is part of the key to understanding its antidote, which follows later. And so, when we arrive in the world of work we have already learned that this strategy works, even if it carries a risk. It can take dramatic forms, as wonderfully illustrated by films like *Disclosure* and *Fatal Attraction*, but before you relax and tell yourself that this is only the stuff of Hollywood, the stories that our clients tell us suggest that it is more common that some of us realize, albeit seldom with critical consequences.

Exposure is being played whenever a persecutor implies to us that they demand our co-operation or else. It is the 'or else' part where the opening move of the game kicks in. Authentic and assertive politics looks to negotiate a WIN/WIN deal, a fair exchange between one favour for another. *Exposure* looks to play WIN/LOSE and that our secret will be revealed. It is imperative that we work to inoculate ourselves and our organizations from the damage that this trick can wreak. In conversation, a mild form might sound start like this...

Ben: 'I hear you are up for the Florida assignment too.'
Lewis: 'Yes ... and let's hope Jerry doesn't find out that you worked at Enron, because it could really affect your chances.'

This only becomes a game when it is used as a coercive and threatening strategy that is played out of self-interest. Perhaps Lewis is afraid that Ben is the better man for the job and feels threatened, and so in order to manipulate events, Lewis plays this game. Perhaps Ben will withdraw his interest in Florida. In our story, *Exposure* is in play in the final e-mail where Surrinder alludes to Jerry having an affair with Ann. Okay it was a bit corny; however, this is based on our experiences and the stories we hear, and regardless of what you think of our ability to write fiction, this Dirty Trick is very real.

Simply put, the game of *Exposure* is a form of organizational blackmail. Whatever information we seek to conceal, for whatever reason, nearly always produces an opportunity for blackmail and exposure by another. Therefore; hiding a big mistake, an indiscretion, your time in therapy or perhaps at AA meetings, an accident, your daughter's drug problems, your over-exaggerated qualifications, your weekend away with Ann Summer *all* provide opportunities for gamey people to exploit through *Exposure*.

GAME STATS: EXPOSURE

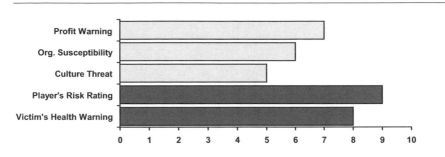

PROFIT WARNING 7/10 (OVERALL, WHAT RISK DOES THIS PRESENT TO THE BOTTOM LINE FOR THE ORGANIZATION?)
Bottom line is that people are doing things they'd rather not have other people know about, and others are using this to warp the decision-making processes of the business. Why? Probably to meet their own ends at the expense of the organization. Therefore, will the business realize its strategy for generating profit for stakeholders? This has big damage potential if it gets out of hand.

ORG. SUSCEPTIBILITY 6/10 (HOW PRONE IS AN ORGANIZATION TO THIS TYPE OF BEHAVIOUR?)
In its mildest form you'd be surprised how often this happens. Frankly, the more macho the organization the more likely it is to be happening. If you've ever been to a party with a sales team you'll know what we mean!

CULTURE THREAT 5/10 (HOW DOES THIS AFFECT THE ORGANIZATION CULTURE, AND STAFF MORALE?)
Overall this trick represents a threat to the integrity of the whole organization. If this becomes pervasive it will quickly lead to a climate of fear and distrust rather than honest good-natured fun. Besides, do you really want these sorts of characters in your organization?

PLAYER'S RISK RATING 9/10 (HOW RISKY IS IT FOR THE PLAYER TO PLAY THIS DIRTY TRICK AND RISK EXPOSURE?)

This is a nasty trick to be using. The victim is painfully aware you are doing it and they may well fight back. Are you squeaky clean? What happens to you if they expose your naïve attempt at blackmail? Is that crime greater than the original offence you were threatening to expose? Not to mention at what point do you overstep the mark and potentially expose yourself to criminal proceedings?

VICTIM'S HEALTH WARNING 8/10 (WHAT RISK IS THE VICTIM PLACED UNDER WHEN THIS TRICK IS IN PLAY?)

Naturally it depends on what you've done that you are afraid of being exposed and what the *Exposer* wants in return for keeping a lid on it. In our experience, the more careless you are about what you get up to, the more you leave yourself open to exploitation from this trick. Sorry to state the obvious.

THE ANTIDOTE: EXPOSURE

Earlier on, we suggested that whatever information you might seek to conceal can produce an opportunity for *Exposure* or blackmail by another. So the first piece of learning is not to get into this game in the first place! Leading a more authentic and open life is easily the best strategy for inoculation. All of which is no consolation if you are currently caught up in this game. However, help is at hand.

Before we go any further please note that the more extreme cases of this game frequently constitute a criminal offence, in which case the person threatening *Exposure* is taking a big risk that they in turn might be exposed by you. If you've got caught in blackmail, seek specialist help. Whatever the degree at which *Exposure* is being played at, the persecutor is gambling on you being so caught up in your own stress and panic that you will fail to notice your personal power in this situation and crucially, just how vulnerable they have made themselves.

Should you find yourself caught up in a less serious variation of this game, which is more about career consequences then there are some tough decisions ahead. You might like to ask yourself the following self-coaching questions before you go any further ...

- What is the real likelihood of them taking this further?
- To what extent am I fantasizing a disastrous outcome?
- Who do I trust to talk this through with, and who can then advise me?
- If they were to do their worst, what power would they have then? What power would I have?
- Is it possible, or perhaps even likely, that they don't want to expose you, because that would neutralize their power?
- How will I feel if I don't take action and just leave things as they are?
- How might I feel if I take action, regardless of the outcome?
- What do I really have to lose if the worst really happens?
- What happens if I just call their bluff and challenge them to do their worst?
- What contingency plans could I put in place to minimize damage?

You might have worked out from the above questions that if you call their bluff and they act on their information and expose you, then their power is most likely at an end. It is also likely that they will damage their own credibility and leave themselves vulnerable. If the worst happens you may well have not only the moral high ground, but power over them. We would encourage you to use this new power wisely and assertively.

There are also some smart questions you can adapt to your particular circumstances to deflect or ward off the *Exposure* player next time they come calling. Choose any or all from the following list to adapt to your own circumstances ...

POWER QUESTIONS TO EXPOSE EXPOSURE ...
- What makes you so confident that this strategy will work?
- What happens if I just call your bluff?
- What makes you think that this is a good way of getting what you want?
- What contingency plans do you suppose I might have made for this situation?

- What do you suppose happens to people who play this game and lose?
- What power will you have left after you have acted on your threat?
- What power might I then have?
- What are the legal consequences for people found guilty of bullying in the workplace?
- What do you suppose might happen next time you need something from me?

Alternatively, you may decide not to give them an opportunity to change their ways. Instead you might decide to just go for it by directly and assertively confronting them about their game playing. In which case it might sound something like this ...

> 'Lewis, I am not prepared to play this game anymore. If you really think that what you are doing is right then go ahead, I am ready to take the consequences. I believe that you know that this is not a great way to get what you want and I would encourage you to cut the crap and chose a better way forward.'

Another strategy is to outflank them. Be honest with those who need to know and come clean, have the difficult conversation and neutralize the power of the *Exposure* player by talking to all the people who need to hear your 'confession'. Go for self-exposure before you are exposed. If you tell the whole story you may well be amazed at how understanding and supportive other people can be, especially if you are any good at what you do professionally. You will then be in a powerful position yourself next time the *Exposure* player comes around. You can then simply tell them that 'the truth is out there' and their power is no more.

Whichever strategy you choose, we know from our work that this is a really tough call and acting assertively to confront them about this game is a risky act and will require both skill and courage. Whatever happens, if you act in line with what we are suggesting you will know that you did the right thing and will most likely emerge stronger for your experience. Remember, the world is a much smaller place now, and what goes around usually comes around sooner rather than later. This is why we want you to end this Dirty Trick now by acting honestly and assertively. We wish you well.

THE POWER OF ...

EXPOSURE

When Machiavellian politicians play games to manipulate us, they are taking a gamble that we will not catch them out, and that even if we did, that we might not be assertive enough to confront them about it. Naming the game is the one thing that Machiavellian politicians are most afraid of. When we name the game we signal our self-confidence, political savvy and our assertiveness. Naming the game is the clearest signal we can send to discourage Machiavelli and warn him off. It might sound something like this...

'What is the real agenda we need to discuss?'
'What is it that you really want from this conversation?'
'What is stopping us from having the real conversation?'
'Let's talk about what is really going on here'
'Cards on the table, what are we really talking about?'
'Is this one of those games where we ...?'
'Is this one of those situations where we ...?'
'I have been listening closely and I wonder what is not being said in this conversation?'

CHAPTER FIVE

A RATHER SAD DISPLAY

The contrast was stark as Ben approached the venue for the strategic away day. With the sun setting ahead of him, Ben drove down the escarpment and into Broadway, a picturesque Cotswold village. Ben marvelled at the pretty cottages, yes even in winter it warmed his heart. After several weeks in a drab and rather wet Luton, perhaps this weekend would not be so bad after all.

Since his fateful meeting with Surrinder, Ben had been busy. So busy that he had even stopped noticing the smell of damp in his squalid guesthouse in Luton. The commute had proved too much and he had resigned himself to staying there during the week. Guesthouse was of course misleading, unless Luton's notion of hospitality included cold breakfasts, undercooked dinners and mould. Health and Safety inspectors clearly thought their own health more important and avoided Luton. He wished he could follow their lead.

His evenings had been spent studying. Following his meeting with Surrinder he had returned to the bookshop and bought several management books, mainly on office politics. He had been rather embarrassed making his purchases, but he was desperate. After seeing all those e-mails, and still reeling from the confusing meetings, he knew he was in a hole, bigger perhaps even than Luton.

As he entered a new world of luxury at the Lygon Arms he had a growing sense of confidence that he had sussed out what was really going on behind the scenes around Genesis. There were a few small gaps but he felt sure that he could fill these during the SAD. Ben was almost looking forward to sitting back and watching the display of moves and games.

'All eyes are now on Luton and we on the Executive Committee are confident that Surrinder, Ben and the rest of the Luton contingent will shortly be reporting to us the rapid progress they have made on bringing in Genesis on time and under budget.' Jerry smiled generously at Surrinder as he concluded a whirlwind presentation that saw him rattle through over thirty PowerPoint slides in the opening 15 minutes of the workshop. As executive sponsor he needed to make an impression.

The rest of the morning Ben relaxed as the attention focused on other big projects. When they broke for lunch he seemed to have reached some conclusions. Which was just as well because he had the first slot after lunch. The significance of the timing was not lost on Ben. The fact that this was usually referred to as the 'graveyard shift' appeared somewhat apt.

Just after lunch, Jerry collared Ben.

'I trust you're not going to let me down!' Jerry opened.

'That rather depends on what you are expecting from me, Jerry.'

'Well I'm afraid if you haven't worked that out by now Ben ...' Jerry paused then changed tack.

'Listen Ben, most people round here just don't think you're up to it. Some even wonder why you were ever employed. They think you just haven't got your head around how things work here and believe you're going to make a hash of things. Not me, I've every confidence in you, Ben.' Jerry moved away quickly before Ben could react, leaving him more than a little unsettled just before his presentation.

Ben had worked hard on his presentation, very hard. He had to be very economical with the words on the slides to ensure that he could get Surrinder to sign it off before the SAD. He also needed to leave himself room to manoeuvre whilst on his feet.

Having been rattled by Jerry, he stood up and got on with the job. He didn't take long. Ben quickly summarized his analysis of the current situation. Reported back on the progress that had been made and summarized his recommendations. Before he could pass out his plans, the MD launched into action.

'Ben, you appear to be saying that London needs to take more responsibility for its actions and I assume you mean that the HR project stream should be completed as originally planned by Lewis.' Before Ben realized that the MD's words were a statement and not a question, Lewis reacted to the direction of JB's stare.

With well-practised nonchalance Lewis responded, 'Well I'm afraid that is just not possible. As you recall I've got more than enough on my plate at the moment what with Project Zeus. Then there is Project …' and so he went on with Jerry smiling at his side. The MD cut into his stream of excuses and fired another statement pretending to be a question at Ben.

'And are you suggesting that overall responsibility for Genesis should be taken by Luton?' Before Ben could work out if he needed to answer, Surrinder fired back at the MD. 'We all know that Sir Bill wanted Jerry to retain responsibility and I for one would not want Jerry feeling like he's losing out here. Jerry is far too critical to the success of Genesis to lose bottom-line accountability.'

'And there's another thing …' Surrinder was on a roll. 'It didn't go unnoticed by everyone that in Jerry's presentation this morning there was a line at the bottom of slide 26 that said that all directors bonus arrangement have been …' she consulted her notes '… realigned to successful implementation of Genesis. When and how was that agreed might I ask?'

As accusations, denials and insults started to fly around the room, Ben marvelled at Surrinder's vigilance. She certainly knew what she was doing. Ben stood quietly at the front of the warring factions, ignored by all and still holding his final handout. It had taken him many very long days to pull together his detailed plans. Now nobody seemed in the least bit interested in his Gantt charts, governance processes and communication strategies. Ben decided to sit in a lonely-looking chair beside the Epson projector and started to wonder what it was like to be an Epson. The things it must have seen over the years.

The MD decided enough was enough. 'Okay, we need to call a halt to this debate. I suggest we take this offline, grab a quick comfort break and then turn our attention to Project Samson.'

By comparison, the remainder of the day was uneventful. The uproar over Genesis had drained the group of any enthusiasm and left a strained atmosphere that could literally be cut with a knife. Ben wondered who would be holding that particular knife.

Unfortunately Ben left the room at the end of the day at the same time as Jerry. Clearly he had some advice for him before they reassembled for dinner. Not a very appetizing prospect and Ben was definitely wishing he could be at home with Hanna on this cold Saturday evening. Somehow he seemed to have proved himself to be a pawn but was now rather confused about whose side he was on. The evening was going to be hell.

'Yes Ben, but you must bear in mind where she, um, comes from,' Jerry whispered to Ben in a conspiratorial tone.

Shocked, Ben retorted 'Surely you are not implying that her race has anything to do with this?'

Jerry momentarily lost his composure with the strength of Ben's reply. It swiftly returned as he leaned in close. 'No, my boy, she's from Luton!'

CHAPTER FIVE: MENTORING INTERVENTION

How many away days to discuss strategy and plans end up like this? Quite a few? Perhaps not too many descending into such chaos, but many end with ambiguous conclusions and no decisions. Away days are also an opportunity for people to play politics, transact power, makes moves, bolster their position and hold many 'secret meetings' to steer things in the way they want them to go. Not to mention of course the manoeuvring that takes place in the run-up to the event. We're confident that you'll know what we mean!

Before we explore the next set of Dirty Tricks, ask yourself a few questions:

- If you were in Ben's shoes, what might you have done differently before the event?
- What appears to be the key issue for Jerry?

- Was Surrinder right to raise the issue about directors' bonus arrangements in this forum?
- Do you sometimes wish you were an Epson projector?
- What is the key issue for Surrinder in this situation?
- Had you been the MD, what would you have done differently?
- Would you like to give up your weekends to have dinner with this crowd?

Maybe not. Now that your radar is starting to get attuned to Dirty Tricks, instead of turning over the page, try to describe the key ones displayed in this chapter. Can you give them a name?

Over the last few years we have built up a catalogue of over 100 such games. This volume covers only 21 so you need to get better at identifying them for yourself, or wait for the next book.

THE DIRTY TRICKS IN CHAPTER FIVE

DIRTY TRICK NO. 13: BURIAL GROUND/DISCOUNT
The tactic of deliberately hiding or obscuring vital information in reports or presentations so that the one critical factor goes unnoticed, and another person or party is duped into making a bad decision or drawing the wrong conclusions.

DIRTY TRICK NO. 14: MALICIOUS FEEDBACK
Deliberately timing the delivery of dishonest, false or critical 'feedback' to deflect, distract or undermine another.

DIRTY TRICK NO. 15: HURRY UP
Avoiding work or responsibility by pretending to be overstretched and overworked.

BURIAL GROUND/
DISCOUNT

The tactic of deliberately hiding or obscuring vital information in reports or presentations so that the one critical factor goes unnoticed, and another person or party is duped into making a bad decision or drawing the wrong conclusions.

This game sometimes occurs when producing legally binding contracts, where one party hides critical, punitive and hugely costly clauses in the small print, in the hope that the buyer can be duped into signing it and therefore end up in a losing position. The old clichés hold true; remember, always read the small print.

Typically when the forced error is discovered the buyer then complains to the seller who, if they chose to continue to be manipulative, then changes the game to a variation of *My Hands are Tied*[1], probably saying something like, 'Sorry Ben, but you signed the contract, there is nothing we can do now' or 'Ben, to get that changed at this stage would mean getting the Legal Department involved again; is that what you really want?'

This trick can be played out in a number of different variations:

1 Where a report is made overly verbose, complex or unstructured with the intention of confusing the reader. This can be done in the hope that the reader will be more likely to make a decision favourable to the author, or simply to hide issues and problems that the author would sooner not have discussed.
2 During a presentation or pitch, the orator skilfully '*Discounts*' critical information by moving quickly, waving aside points or simply omitting to discuss points relevant to the decision in hand.

Papers sent ahead of a key meeting are ripe for this trick. Sometimes papers are presented at short notice and are often very long. Obviously the information has to be conveyed, but too often little thought is given to a structure that optimizes the decision-making process for key people. Honest, clear and comprehensive communication is necessary. This does not make it a trick.

However if there is a deliberate attempt to disguise or hide the critical information, or simply sending huge reports too close to a decisive meeting for accurate understanding, then this becomes a classic Dirty Trick at work. For instance, if all bar one of the key issues/concerns are summarized at the beginning of the paper, the other being buried in the detail, it's a game. If there is no executive summary, be on your guard, or if it

---

[1] See Chapter Seven.

arrives on your desk an hour before the meeting, watch out. Note that when spotting this trick, some people are not guilty of deception; they just may be inept communicators. Despite this, your vigilance is still required.

In Chapter Five we are witness to the *Discount* variation of this trick during Jerry's initial presentation. Surrinder is nobody's fool however, and picks it up easily. Perhaps Jerry has done this too many times before and Surrinder, knows to be on her guard. Jerry appears to have wanted to hide the fact that a decision had been made to link Genesis responsibility to bonuses. Too bad Jerry, she noticed!

GAME STATS: BURIAL GROUND/DISCOUNT

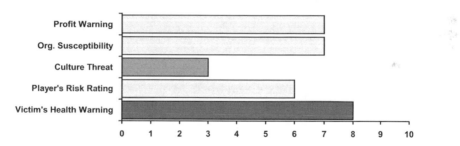

PROFIT WARNING 7/10 (OVERALL, WHAT RISK DOES THIS PRESENT TO THE BOTTOM LINE FOR THE ORGANIZATION?)
If this trick is in play, it is highly likely that there are some serious issues being decided and which will clash with the Machiavellian manager's personal agenda. If key business decisions are not made with all the relevant facts, then the cost to the business could be huge.

ORG. SUSCEPTIBILITY 7/10 (HOW PRONE IS AN ORGANIZATION TO THIS TYPE OF BEHAVIOUR?)
Surprisingly frequent. Particularly with projects that are not going too well, and where

someone has something to hide, usually their incompetence or the extent to which they will profit personally from a deal. It never ceases to amaze us just how reluctant people are to admit their mistakes. Instead they just try to cover things up with this trick.

CULTURE THREAT 3/10 (HOW DOES THIS AFFECT THE ORGANIZATION CULTURE, AND STAFF MORALE?)
A relatively low threat really. The main impact on the culture is a growing tendency to produce over-long confusing reports and fast busy presentations.

PLAYER'S RISK RATING 6/10 (HOW RISKY IS IT FOR THE PLAYER TO PLAY THIS DIRTY TRICK AND RISK EXPOSURE?)
More of an embarrassment factor if exposed. As we saw in this chapter, Jerry played the trick and got exposed. This threw his plans and the meeting into chaos. So Jerry didn't gain. If the omission is serious this could even lead to criminal proceedings. Notice the increasing investigations in the public sector concerning disclosure of information.

VICTIM'S HEALTH WARNING 8/10 (WHAT RISK IS THE VICTIM PLACED UNDER WHEN THIS TRICK IS IN PLAY?)
If someone is playing this it stands to reason that if they succeed you are going to lose out. Given that this usually happens with serious matters, be very much on your guard.

THE ANTIDOTE: BURIAL GROUND/DISCOUNT

It is of course better to ensure that we do not invite people to play this game with us in the first place. We can, at least in part, inoculate ourselves by being clear about specific vital criteria that we want explicitly highlighted, so that we can see it and understand it. Sadly this is not always possible especially if we are in a position where we don't know what it is that we don't know!

To reduce the risk of this trick being used, be very clear about your expectations and how you want them to report back or present. Choose any or all of the following:

- Be clear about the questions you need to have answered.
- Insist that each is answered in the report succinctly.
- Insist on an executive summary that covers all the important points.
- Ask them to get other key questions from key stakeholders.
- Clarify what decision needs to be taken. Then determine what information is required. Get them to lay this out clearly.
- Suggest that they also present the counter-arguments so that the audience can see both sides.
- Get them to consider 'all' the options, not just their favoured one!

We're sure you can think of more points along these lines that will help to minimize the risk of this trick arising in the first place.

When we find ourselves in the middle of a bewildering presentation, or discussing a confusing report, try some of the questions and watch the reactions closely. These questions are all designed to invite the other party into behaving more honestly and authentically with us from the outset. They won't guarantee success, but at least we will be able to say that we gave them the chance to be clear.

POWER QUESTIONS TO DIG AROUND IN THE BURIAL GROUND
- What are all the important factors that I need to know about?
- What is it that I don't know about this yet?
- What is the one question that I need to ask you that so far I have not?
- What possible pitfalls could you tell me about at this stage?
- My concerns are these ... to what extent will these be explicitly addressed?
- What information might your report be holding back?
- What do I need to know that we have yet to discuss?
- If you wanted to kill this idea, what question would you ask?
- What potential reasons are there for going against your recommendation?

- What is it that you know that I don't know?
- What is the one question that you suggest I most need to ask at this stage?
- What, if anything, might you be tempted to hold back, fudge or hide?

At the very least, this will put someone on the spot. How they react will speak volumes. Irrespective of a trick being in play, these are pretty good questions to use.

If you have been caught out by this game, (in other words, you now know what it is that you didn't know!) you need to make sure it doesn't happen again. Our suggested strategy to do this involves letting the Machiavellian manager know clearly and assertively that you know that this is a game they have been playing. Not to let them know that you now know what has been going on signals a lack of assertion on your part, and provides a beacon to Machiavelli that this tactic works. Furthermore that you are not impressed and more importantly that you will not be putting up with doing business like this in the future. All this needs to be done with tact and skill so as to ensure that we invite the other person into being honest and motivate them toward building more authentic ways of doing business in the future.

> 'Jerry, you knew the information that I needed to know in order to make the right decision, so you will know that I am really disappointed that this one vital piece was buried/omitted. In order for the best decisions to be made for the good of our customers, we need all of the relevant facts. Now how about we talk constructively about how we can avoid this in the future?'

Of course, you may choose to highlight the damage the omission caused. When you do this, we strongly suggest that this happens early, is succinct, and that you move quickly on to the proposals to improve the way you work together. This element of providing a way forward for the future is vital as it signals our political savvy and suggests we are interested in working productively with them in the future. Adversaries we do not need to collect!

If none of this works, remember that you probably have some choice about who to deal with, and you can decide to take your custom elsewhere. If you are in an unfortunate position where you can't go elsewhere, then at least you are forewarned about this individual and will know to be on your guard for the next time.

Now you've got to decide if this battle is strategically important enough to fight. It frequently is. You also need to determine how best to adapt this strategy to meet your specific needs. We know this is a challenge (if it was easy to confront this game would never get played), but it is probably vital that you at least take heart and give it a go! Whatever the outcome, you'll have signalled to them that you are politically intelligent, and that you are assertive and honest. Our experience is that you'll actually gain an awful lot more.

THE POWER OF ...

STRATEGY AND CHOICE

Okay, so someone is playing a game, they might have even got one over on you, and you probably feel like getting revenge! Whilst revenge is a natural human reaction and motivation, it is not always such a great move as revenge usually exacerbates the situation and leads to escalation. Yes, there is an assertive way forward, but pull back from taking immediate action and ask yourself if this is a battle that is really worth it. Choosing your battles strategically is important. Given the level of political activity in organizations it is just not possible to win every political battle, so save your energy and talent for the really important issues and let the small stuff go. Is this political battle one that is vital for you to win? Sometimes it will be better to let Machiavelli have a little victory as you have more important things to do.

DIRTY TRICK NO. 14:

MALICIOUS FEEDBACK

Deliberately timing the delivery of dishonest, false or critical 'feedback' to deflect, distract or undermine another.

'Feedback is the breakfast of champions[2]'. Which is, of course, true provided the feedback is given honestly and constructively, and is designed to help us to move forward more productively. Genuine feedback needs to be treated like a gift; we should listen carefully even if we do not like what we hear. Sadly however, 'feedback' can also be used for manipulative purposes. The trick of *Malicious Feedback* is played by giving someone misleading feedback, which is intended to be unhelpful, rather than helpful, affirming and furthering our development.

Unfortunately, not everyone has our best interests at heart. Some people have their own agenda and frequently see the need to make use of this Dirty Trick to help them. When someone says, 'Let me give you some feedback', you might need to be on your guard! At best this might be code for 'incoming critical message ahoy'. At worst it is a game about giving us misleading, inaccurate or erroneous feedback, with the intention of distracting us or deflecting us from our purpose.

The difficult part is how to recognize when this trick is in play. Usually *Malicious Feedback* is vague and attributed to other unnamed individuals. Rarely will it be from the person giving the feedback. Whilst there may be some element of truth, it is carefully manipulated either in nature or impact.

For example, we recently worked with a highly talented young manager who had been seconded to an important project team. He discovered that there were some serious flaws in the project work and found that he was able to make a huge contribution by asking all the difficult questions that no one else seemed to notice should be being asked. After a few weeks his line manager summoned him to a meeting and gave him the 'feedback' he had received from the project manager which was to stop *'rocking the boat and asking so many questions'*. Notice firstly that the feedback did not come directly from the project manager, but arrived in a roundabout fashion. He told us that the impact that this feedback had on him was that it knocked his self-confidence, sent the message that his managers had been colluding behind his back and he was confused because he was earnest and wanted to do the best he could for the project. At sub-

---

[2] Attributed to a number of people including Ken Blanchard, Tony Robbins and Rick Tate. Whoever said it first, top marks!

sequent meetings he kept his guard and held back on his reservations and questions, to the detriment of the project. When we heard his story we asked him if it was possible that his talent and intellect had been inadvertently making the project manager and his project team members appear in a bad light. Only then did he appreciate that being good is not always going to be good enough in the world of work, and that his political skills would need to be improved.

Direct *Malicious Feedback* is delivered by the Machiavellian manager directly and is often about timing, the feedback being delivered at the worst possible moment for you, inviting you into feeling bad or threatening your concentration or confidence. In our story, we see Jerry deliberately attempting to unsettle Ben just before he takes the graveyard shift for his critical presentation to the SAD. He also generalized about the feedback coming from unnamed others; however, he engages in the trick directly with Ben. He carefully and strongly denied that he thought the same, creating more confusion. And the timing could not have been worse for Ben. Jerry also failed to give Ben an opportunity to understand more, another telltale sign that the game is in play.

Before you start seeing *Malicious Feedback* everywhere remember that this Dirty Trick should not be confused with incompetence. Despite the millions that are spent every year on developing managers' ability to provide good feedback we are regularly depressed by the relatively low level of skill displayed. The good news is that our advice on handling this trick will help deal with incompetence as well as game playing. So take heart!

GAME STATS: MALICIOUS FEEDBACK

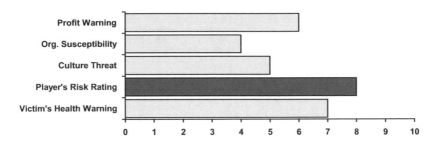

PROFIT WARNING 6/10 (OVERALL, WHAT RISK DOES THIS PRESENT TO THE BOTTOM LINE FOR THE ORGANIZATION?)
The main risk this presents when played is that it starts to disarm the opposition to someone's personal agenda. If this agenda is not aligned for the good of the organization then a hit on the profitability of the business is likely.

ORG. SUSCEPTIBILITY 4/10 (HOW PRONE IS AN ORGANIZATION TO THIS TYPE OF BEHAVIOUR?)
Overall this trick is usually played on small things, albeit frequently. The more malicious variant is not too common, partly because the risk of exposure is so high.

CULTURE THREAT 5/10 (HOW DOES THIS AFFECT THE ORGANIZATION CULTURE, AND STAFF MORALE?)
Malicious Feedback is often recognized at some point. When that point arrives in the mind of the individual it causes suspicion and distrust. If this becomes widespread it will have a significant impact on the culture of the organization.

PLAYER'S RISK RATING 8/10 (HOW RISKY IS IT FOR THE PLAYER TO PLAY THIS DIRTY TRICK AND RISK EXPOSURE?)
If you play this game the risk of exposure is very high because the victim will draw conclusions. They may not be fully aware of the malicious intent, but they will certainly be feeling antipathy towards you and are unlikely to trust your 'feedback' in future. If you are unlucky enough to play it on someone who's read the antidote below, watch out!

VICTIM'S HEALTH WARNING 7/10 (WHAT RISK IS THE VICTIM PLACED UNDER WHEN THIS TRICK IS IN PLAY?)
How thick is your skin? If you can take criticism well and are strong and confident you are probably not going to be too affected by this, even though it is unpleasant. Conversely, if you are still learning, or are new in your job, this trick can have a dramatic negative effect on your performance. Unfortunately it is all too easy for this to develop into a vicious circle as the feedback starts to become reality.

THE ANTIDOTE: MALICIOUS FEEDBACK

The motive behind this trick is to unsettle you, deflect your concentration, reduce your confidence, or to increase the likelihood that you'll make a hash of something important. Underneath this can be a desire to be one up at your expense or to undermine your performance at a critical moment. *Malicious Feedback* either comes to you directly from the Machiavellian manager, or indirectly from someone who is the messenger, perhaps well intentioned, acting on Machiavelli's behalf. Consequently there are two ways to tackle this Dirty Trick, depending on the level of directness.

INDIRECT MALICIOUS FEEDBACK (WHERE PERHAPS A WELL-MEANING MANAGER OR COLLEAGUE GIVES YOU FEEDBACK THEY ARE PASSING ON FROM ANOTHER)
The first step towards an effective antidote is to keep your emotional intelligence switched on, to remain calm and objective. Because *Malicious Feedback* engages your sense of unfairness and is ego damaging, your emotions are likely to be easily engaged.

Our second step is to get curious rather than angry. Ask the messenger smart questions to raise your collective awareness about what might really be going on, which gently probes and challenges the validity of the feedback. The good thing with this tactic is that you don't have to be certain at this stage if there is a Dirty Trick in progress; specifics always help. When the opportunity is right, ask them lots of questions with a spirit of honest enquiry. Use the questions below to inspire and prompt you.

POWER QUESTIONS TO ASK THE INDIRECT FEEDBACK MESSENGER
- Can you be more specific about the feedback?
- What are the facts?
- Where does it come from?
- When did you pick up this feedback?
- Can you give me examples that led to this feedback?
- Who else is involved in producing this feedback?
- What do you think is the intention behind this feedback?
- What did Jerry actually say? What were his exact words?
- What should I be doing differently in the light of this feedback?
- How should I use this feedback to benefit the department/organization etc?
- Why did I not get this feedback directly from the person who raised it?
- What stopped Jerry from giving me this feedback himself?
- To what extent do you agree with the feedback?
- Which aspects do you support?
- Which elements do you think are erroneous?
- I would like to hear this direct from Jerry. What do you think his response would be?

The responses we get to these questions will inform us of the extent to which a game is in progress. We might want to go further. This requires strength and commitment and should be reserved for moments when we are sure that the indirect feedback is indeed malicious, and we want to stop it happening again. People we have worked with have found real benefit from statements along the lines of:

'Surrinder, I suspect that this feedback is really designed to stop me asking difficult questions at the project meeting. I'd appreciate us having a more detailed conversation, so let's talk about what is really going on here and how best we can manage the situation.'

Additionally, you could seek out and assertively confront Jerry about his motives for providing this feedback so indirectly. This is to clearly signal to Machiavelli our self-confidence, our unwillingness to be manipulated and the extent of our political savvy. With all of our direct interventions, they need to be delivered assertively and with emotions under control. Also notice that this intervention ends with the invitation to work together more co-operatively. Machiavelli won't always respond to this invitation, but at least we have signalled our positive intent and this helps to keep us on the moral high ground. Putting it all together it might sound something like this:

'Jerry, Surrinder has given me your feedback. I'm a little disappointed you did not speak to me directly and I wonder why that was the case? I want this project to be a success, so let's have an open conversation about what is really going on here and find a better way forward.'

The key advantage you have with indirect *Malicious Feedback* is that time is on your side. You do not need to act in the heat of the moment and can use this time to sense check and pressure test your ideas for moving forward with positive politics and integrity intact.

DIRECT MALICIOUS FEEDBACK
An example of direct *Malicious Feedback* (unhelpful feedback coming directly from a Machiavellian adversary) might go something like this:

'Ben, about your presentation today; I've been chatting to the chaps and, well, I think it is a shame that Sir Bill thinks your project is a dead duck and that JB thinks you are not up to the job, but hey, good luck!'

Again, the first thing you need to do is to take steps to avoid becoming emotional. Remember that the motive is probably to upset and undermine you, so any inappropriate emotional display assures Machiavelli that the tactic is working and reinforces their belief that you can be manipulated in this way. If at all possible give yourself the opportunity to think it through before you respond. One way to achieve this is to simply hear out their feedback, thank them for their view and as soon as possible move away and retreat to think things through. *'Thanks Jerry, I'd like to pick this up again after my session. Perhaps then we will have time to talk about the specifics so I can understand exactly what you have to say'*. Once out of reach of Machiavelli, coach yourself using the following questions to cut through the emotions and get focused on effective ways forward.

- What was really being said?
- What is their real motive?
- How else could this feedback be interpreted?
- What other agenda's might be behind this feedback?
- How significant is this feedback really?
- What might be significant about the timing of this feedback?
- How likely is it that someone is just trying to put me off my stroke?
- What happens if I just ignore this feedback?
- What is the bigger picture that I need to keep in mind?
- Who would be the best person to deliver any response to?
- When would be a good time to respond to what has been said?
- Putting emotion to one side, what would an appropriate and effective response be?

The bottom line for you right now is to make good decisions about what to do next, to keep calm and controlled and regardless of the Machiavellian antics, go and do a great job. Becoming deflected, distracted or deflated is to hand Machiavelli the victory he craves.

Later on you might decide that it is worth confronting Machiavelli about their feedback. This can be helpful if done with positive political skill as it again demonstrates our confidence, that we will not be deflected from our purpose and that we are politically savvy. It sends a clear and positive message to Machiavelli that we are not to be manipulated in this way. It might sound something like this:

> 'Jerry, I want to talk about the feedback that you gave me just before the meeting. The information and timing could have been an unhelpful distraction, so I wonder what was on your mind when you delivered it?'

Machiavelli won't always be invited into working with integrity and an admission is unlikely; however, we have clearly signalled that we are not to be tripped up in this way and we diminish the likelihood that he will try this trick with us again.

So now it is over to you to decide how best to adapt this strategy to meet your specific needs. Intervening in this game is not easy, but having made the decision to act and giving it your best shot, you'll have signalled that you are politically astute. Our experience is that you can't win them all, but you have increased your chances of a successful outcome by acting assertively.

THE POWER OF ...

THE INNER GAME

The inner game refers to your own internal dialogue. The part of your brain that automatically coaches and encourages you, that nurtures you and gives you the occasional pep talk. Unfortunately it is also the same voice that carps and complains about your performance. It can even become an unending stream of whispered and unhelpful messages that needs to be controlled. In a sales situation, an unhelpful inner dialogue might sound something like this.

'Just listen to yourself, do you really believe what you are saying? They'll never fall for that, surely.'

'You're tying yourself in knots here, try using English as a first language why don't you!'

'Look at him, he's not buying this at all. That was the wrong thing to say, he's switched off now.'

'This always happens when you pitch it like this, when will you learn! You've lost this opportunity, now the boss will be furious.'

'Perhaps you should change tack, this isn't working. If you don't make this sale you'll never make budget.'

If you gain control of your inner voice you will immediately become more power-ful.

DIRTY TRICK NO. 15

HURRY UP

Avoiding work or responsibility by pretending to be overstretched and over-worked.

Have you noticed how rare it is to find someone who is not busy? Most of us need to feel we're adding value by the bucket load. Also the idle employee needs to watch out lest redundancy is just around the corner!

Some of us have a *Hurry Up* working style whereby we feel a need to be constantly working at a high pace, and when things slow down we feel we are somehow making a lesser contribution, regardless of quality or output. This is not a Dirty Trick, just a psychological working style that needs appreciating and understanding. However, some people deliberately create a perception of busyness to avoid taking responsibility or getting landed with problematic or unpleasant tasks. They dash around the office, phone permanently attached to ear, claiming to be overworked, stretched or pressured, and frequently clutching a document or project folder plucked from a desk that looks like a bomb has hit it. The energy they exert in avoiding work often produces a whirlwind of activity whilst actually achieving very little for the team, the organization, and ironically, themselves. A recent TV advert showed a young man emerging from the pub at closing time, going back to the office where he fell asleep at his desk, specifically to be seen by his boss arriving at 07.30 who then assumed he had been working all night!

The *Hurry Up* player believes that they are impressing important people with the extent of their commitment and hard work. Sometimes they are right and some managers do fall for it. They might also be attempting to manipulate others into feeling guilty about how slowly they are responding, how little they themselves are achieving and the fact that they seldom seem to offer assistance to the *Hurry Up* player. In short this game is frequently played as an invitation to others to feel bad as much as a strategy for avoiding more work or resistance.

A variant of *Hurry Up* that needs to be watched out for is where often a more senior manager claims to be too busy, which is a cover for 'I'm not interested in your proposition'. This is closely allied to *Tell Me More*, which we covered in Chapter Two.

The roots of the *Hurry Up* trick are often found early in their career. They have found that by behaving like this they avoid trouble and get help from others. The attention this brings usually bolsters their feelings of self-importance and proves, to them at least, just how critical they are to the organization.

In our story, when the MD rounds on Lewis he is met with a barrage of typical *Hurry Up* excuses. He is offered plausible reasons why he is too busy to take on work. In reality he views this work as career-threatening. However, we doubt very much that Lewis rushes around the office in a whirlwind of inactivity, he's far too polished for that.

Of course many people are genuinely overworked. However, the antidote advice which follows will help you and them to find a way of sifting through their priorities or agreeing that they are indeed simply too busy.

GAME STATS: HURRY UP

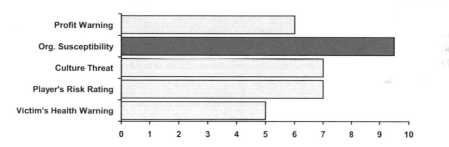

PROFIT WARNING 6/10 (OVERALL, WHAT RISK DOES THIS PRESENT TO THE BOTTOM LINE FOR THE ORGANIZATION?)
The bottom line is that when you have people playing *Hurry Up* you have unproductive people, or people who should be taking more responsibility, or more likely both. This can seriously affect the delivery capability of your business and damage productivity and profitability.

ORG. SUSCEPTIBILITY 9.5/10 (HOW PRONE IS AN ORGANIZATION TO THIS TYPE OF BEHAVIOUR?)
Rare indeed is the organization that does not have this trick in play by large numbers of people.

CULTURE THREAT 7/10 (HOW DOES THIS AFFECT THE ORGANIZATION CULTURE, AND STAFF MORALE?)
If you want a culture that is 'can do, will do' this trick needs addressing. The cultural threat is that if too widespread, getting things done will start to feel more like wading through treacle.

PLAYER'S RISK RATING 7/10 (HOW RISKY IS IT FOR THE PLAYER TO PLAY THIS DIRTY TRICK AND RISK EXPOSURE?)
The risk you run depends on the number of authentic high performers you have around you. If your behaviour is out of line with the majority, you face a high penalty by playing this trick. Not only will your performance be disregarded, you'll also find respect dwindling the more you use this trick.

VICTIM'S HEALTH WARNING 5/10 (WHAT RISK IS THE VICTIM PLACED UNDER WHEN THIS TRICK IS IN PLAY?)
Although frustrating, the *Hurry Up* player is fairly easy to pin down if you follow the antidote advice below. If left unchecked however, you will start to falter in your own performance as you struggle to overcome the resistance and your work–life balance is eroded because you've got to do more for yourself.

THE ANTIDOTE: HURRY UP

The first step towards an antidote is to understand the motivations of the *Hurry Up* player. You need to determine as best you can if they are employing this tactic to either make you feel bad, avoid doing work (or taking responsibility) or as a resistance strategy. The advice that follows will assist you irrespective of whether or not a Dirty Trick is in play.

FEEL BAD

To recognize this motive, you need to be alert to what they are saying and when they are saying it. Should they regularly puff and blow about how busy they are without any threat of extra work from you, chances are they're playing *Hurry Up* to make you feel bad and hopefully get your help. The puzzling aspect of this behaviour is that rather than simply ask for help they seem set on leaving you to eventually work out what they want. We suspect that part of the reason for this is that they also want you to feel sorry for them, which in itself is a pay-off. The telltale clue of this additional pay-off is the harried look they have perfected.

The antidote for this one is easy. As a human being you, and only you, are in charge of your own thoughts, feelings and behaviours, therefore you can simply decide that you are not going to be manipulated into feeling guilty, awkward, slow, ineffective etc. Easier said than done, but we suggest you practise this objective stance. Once you have made this decision, provide them with constructive help by using some of the tips below. When they realize that you are not going to fall for it, the questions below will assist them in making some good choices about how to work with you in future.

AVOIDING WORK/RESPONSIBILITIES

If you suspect that avoidance is the motivation behind *Hurry Up*, the way you handle this depends on your power relationship with the player. If you have direct authority over the individual you are partly responsible if they are too busy. In which case you should approach this as a coach and mentor. With more evenly matched power, mutual co-operation is often the best attitude to adopt until such time as you have increased your power so you can take a tougher line. Perhaps the most difficult situation is when you clearly have much less power than the *Hurry Up* player. In this case we suggest you tackle this in a respectful but firm manner.

When you need something done and you get *Hurry Up* in response, you need to start asking questions. The questions below are suggestions and you need to pick those that are appropriate to the relationship. The way you deliver these will also be dependent on this power dynamic, so choose carefully.

POWER QUESTIONS TO ASK A HURRY UP AVOIDING WORK
If you have more power ...
- What progress are you making against each of your objectives?
- Recap on what timescales are you working to?
- Specifically where have you got to do with Project Zeus?
- How are you measuring your output?
- What have you actually achieved today (week and month)?
- How are you feeling about your workload?
- How are you feeling about the progress you are making?
- What is your biggest time stealer?
- To what extent are these constraints real or imaginary?
- What are the real priorities that you need to focus on?

If there is an even power balance ...
- Why are you too busy?
- How does this compete with your other priorities?
- What is stopping you doing this right now?
- How does this work fit with your longer term plans?
- In what ways would you benefit by making this a priority?
- Who is preventing you from agreeing to do this work?
- What would you have to stop doing to be able to do this?

If you have less power ...
- How does this fit with your other priorities?
- What do you need from me to be able to schedule this task?
- How can I help make it easy for you to do this?
- When will you be able to do it?
- Is there any other reason for not being able to do this?
- Could it be the case that you just don't want to do this?

One of the great things about this is that whatever attempts you make to ask these questions, you don't have to complete your mission in one meeting. You can come back and ask more. The answers to the questions above, and others that you think are appropriate will help you to understand more about the reality of the situation the player (or rather busy person) is facing. Moreover they will equip you with knowledge to improve your ability to influence them in the future.

Not interested

The final variant worth mentioning is the one where you suspect that they are using the trick of *Hurry Up* to cover their real position. Often they believe that what you are asking them to do is not worthwhile, or is a waste of their time and energy. When they play *Hurry Up* they are telling a lie very similar to that of *Tell Me More* (see Chapter Two). Re-read the antidote advice for that Dirty Trick and modify the approach to fit this trick. Some additional questions may help you.

POWER QUESTIONS TO ASK THE UNINTERESTED HURRY UP
- What other reasons are there for not doing this now?
- Why is this not high on your agenda?
- What would it take to put this top of your priorities?
- What reasons are there for ditching this task?
- Do you think I should be spending my time on this?
- What are you uncertain about with what I am asking for?

The responses you get to these questions will tell you much about the individual and the way they like to do things. Based on the advice in many of the other antidotes we think you'll now be in a position to get much tougher if you feel it is appropriate to do so.

THE POWER OF ...

CHARM, GOOD MANNERS AND CONSIDERATION
You cannot account for how Machiavelli will behave or respond when you confront them about their dirty politics. Everyone, even Machiavelli, has a right to their own thoughts, feelings and behaviour, and they need to take responsibility for that. But what you can do is to invite them into a more productive dialogue by good interpersonal skills. Being polite, courteous, respectful and in control in these situations, increases your personal power rather than diminishes it. Those managers who think that a 'damn good ticking-off' will help, are usually deluding themselves, and what usually lurks behind this is a misplaced macho desire to be seen to be powerful. Theirs is a primitive strategy. You can make the choice and behave like a human being, and they can keep banging the rocks together and swinging in the trees!

CHAPTER SIX

A DAY AT THE BELFRY

'Well, at least it's not on my budget' Ben commented to Lewis as they strolled out onto the fairway at The Belfry on a rather crisp December morning. Rather a pleasant change from a damp Luton.

'Hmm ...' Lewis replied with a slight smile. This did not go unnoticed by Ben and he made a mental note to take a careful look at the next Genesis variance report.

This was pure indulgence. Not even an attempt to make it look like a customer day. There were none in sight and as far as Ben knew, none had been invited. 'For senior managers only' the invite had read. Lewis had mentioned that it was one of only two events in the Xennic calendar that were culturally obligatory, the other being the Christmas Ball. Ben was concerned about this waste of money for two reasons. Firstly, Genesis was underfunded and his efforts to get even a little bit more had proved fruitless. Secondly, he was rubbish at golf. Having said that, at least it was not a weekend event for a change.

Whilst Lewis made a show of selecting his club to tee off, Ben reflected back on the SAD. After the rumpus caused by his presentation he had left with more than a little trepidation. What had followed however was even more shocking.

Silence. Okay it was only last weekend and today was Thursday, but he hadn't even been summoned by Surrinder. No angry calls from Jerry; not even an e-mail, which was highly unusual. His inbox was noticeably light on new messages. Something must be happening, but what? At the end of the day the MD had concluded by stating that all decisions arising would be resolved and cast in stone at the forthcoming board meeting, which was next Monday. Ben was jolted from his reflections when the MD strode up and interrupted Lewis as he approached the tee.

'Lewis, where's Surrinder?'

'Oh, hello JB, how are you?' Lewis replied.

'Never mind that, where is Surrinder?'

'I thought Jerry had told you.'

'Told me what exactly?'

Lewis frowned as he realized that once again he was doing Jerry's dirty work. Why was it always left to him? Lewis was proud of the fact that the great man himself, and great in so many ways, would be nothing if it was not for his continued efforts. Navigating the shadowy side of Xennic was his speciality. He particularly favoured the job of lurking behind office partitions eavesdropping. The real power behind the throne. And without doubt indispensable to Jerry and the smooth working of Xennic.

'To be totally honest with you, Jerry is very worried about her,' Lewis began.

'Why?'

'Well, with what has been going on lately, he is concerned that she is putting herself under too much pressure.'

'Then a day out in the fresh air would do her good.'

'Well no ...' Lewis was calculating: 'a little bird told me that she had confided her marriage is on the rocks as well, partly because ...' Lewis paused for effect '... well, you know what she's like with the ...'

The MD cut in gruffly 'So Jerry didn't invite her.'

Lewis, stunned, could only utter an affirmative as JB stalked off. It was not one of his better moments. As he prepared to tee off he seemed somewhat distracted as he struggled with a recovery strategy.

Ben was a little amused at this exchange. It was nice to see Lewis being outgunned. Despite his smooth delivery and skilful articulation, the power of the MD was obvious. He was a man in command and clearly not a very happy man today. Ben suppressed a smile as Lewis drove the ball into the rough.

Jerry was a real pro on the golf course. What surprised Ben was that Lewis and he were catching him up. As they arrived at the 8th green Jerry was having an intense conversation with one of the other senior executives. As Ben came within earshot of the pair he caught the end of a question from Jerry.

'… so I can count on you old chap?'

'Yes Jerry, I suppose so, but that makes us even, okay?'

Jerry seemed startled when he realized they had company. He grasped the executives' elbow and quickly started to move him away from Ben and Lewis whilst frowning at Ben. Somewhere deep in Ben's mind he made a link between Jerry, The Belfry, bats and demonic ogres.

'What was all that about, Lewis?' Ben enquired.

'Come on Ben, you must know how things work around here by now?' Lewis smiled conspiratorially.

'No, do tell.'

Lewis would not be drawn however as he prepared for his putt. Clearly things were going on and whilst he had not been privy to anything over the last week, moves were being made to resolve the problems. Lewis steadied, pulled back his putter and as he brought it towards the ball his concentration was ruined by a rather loud and tinny rendition of 'Land of Hope and Glory'. His ball missed the hole completely and he glared round for the offending owner of the mobile phone.

The MD was oblivious to Lewis's consternation as he stalked away with his phone glued to his ear. Unbeknown to the other golfers, the call was from the HR Director whose absence at The Belfry had been unexplained until now. He had phoned JB to tell him that he had been called back to the office to deal with an urgent matter. This involved a visit from a very calm Surrinder who wanted to inform him that she had just filed a claim of racial discrimination against Xennic. It all appeared to revolve around

Jerry. JB was not amused as he let the golfers know he'd decided to call it a day and head for the 19th hole.

To Ben it had been an interesting morning. Not least because with so many other things going on, nobody seemed to be too interested in his failings on the fairway. Instead they focused on any number of informal meetings between the greens. As they left the 18th green, Ben spotted Jerry striding towards him.

'Hello Ben, need to have a quick chat. I've got a development opportunity for you.' Ben's political radar started flashing.

'Of course it's up to you, but we've got a project that needs a firm hand in Cumbernauld. Lovely Scottish town. This could be just the thing you need right now. Usual stuff, limited budget, way behind schedule. Just up your street in fact.'

Ben was well aware of what street that would be. The reputation of Cumbernauld differed somewhat from Jerry's view[1]. Smiling, Ben replied, 'Tell me more ...'

'Not much more to say really, but there is an alternative. I've been thinking that we really ought to extend your responsibilities on Genesis. If you don't want Cumbernauld you'll have to take full responsibility for all of the London actions, starting at the board meeting next week. Anyway, let me know tomorrow first thing will you? And remember, you still report to me.' With that, Jerry strode off to find the MD in the clubhouse.

Lewis smiled and turned the knife. 'Cumbernauld, how would your wife react to that one eh?' Ben knew the answer.

CHAPTER SIX: MENTORING INTERVENTION

Xennic is starting to move towards the end game of this political episode. Ben appears more confident and even enjoys a little 'in-joke' with Jerry at the end, albeit only for

---

[1] Cumbernauld was awarded the Carbuncle Award in 2001 for 'the most dismal place in Scotland'. Along with other such awards, in February 2005 its citizens begged Channel 4 'for dynamite and bulldozers to deliver them oblivion'. We await Channel 4's decision with interest; from a safe distance.

our consumption. We suspect that you are also starting to become well tuned-in to the moves being made.

   Here are some questions for you to ponder:

- What consequences does Surrinder's claim bring to Xennic?
- Can you describe the plot behind our story?
- Is Jerry in serious trouble? Why?
- Would you like your town demolished by Channel 4?
- If you were Ben, what would you have done differently?
- What reactions do you think you would have got from these changes?
- Can you think of a better ring tone for JB?

If you didn't take the time to try to work out the tricks in the last chapter we'd like to reiterate that this is a critical part of building your political intelligence. Try to write down the Dirty Tricks on display in Chapter Six before you turn over. Extra points awarded for thinking of good names.

THE DIRTY TRICKS IN CHAPTER SIX

DIRTY TRICK NO. 16: NO INVITATION
The tactic of leaving people off distribution lists so they miss important meetings or information.

DIRTY TRICK NO. 17: THE CAUCUS
Coercing people behind the scenes before an important meeting or debate.

DIRTY TRICK NO. 18: ROCK AND A HARD PLACE
Manipulating people by offering limited or fixed choices expecting the victim to choose the lesser of two evils.

DIRTY TRICK NO. 16
NO INVITATION

The tactic of leaving people off distribution lists so they miss important meetings or information.

With the growth of virtual teams, cross-discipline working parties, steering committees and matrix reporting this situation is on the increase. Mistakes will happen, it's a fact. Sometimes people get confused or are tardy and forget to let people know about important meetings and forums they should attend. There is also the problem of organizations pushing back on unnecessary e-mails. All of these factors lead to a great many genuine reasons why you were missed off the list.

This becomes a Dirty Trick when someone is missed off deliberately. There can be any number of reasons for this. Perhaps the persecutor would be blown off course if you attended the meeting. Maybe they want to keep you away from the powerful others who will be present, thereby removing the risk that you will impress them with your ideas and presence. If you represent competition to their ambitions, keeping you out of the way helps to give them room to make their moves.

On a more sinister angle, the motive could be to prevent you from finding out information critical to your mission. Their hope could be that you will falter having missed hearing other people's views, their important input or the chance for you to influence decisions. This is particularly likely if you are opposed to their agenda. Alternatively, if you are kept out of the loop you will perhaps be on the sidelines of any decisions taken, or could be embarrassed at having missed such a critical meeting.

Perhaps the most common scenario is when you are new to an existing team or project. The established members may be wary of your presence. They will wonder what your agenda is or may already know that you are going to be presenting a view which conflicts with the constitution. Part of the social processes involved in work teams is a period during which the group will assess your suitability to become part of the team, albeit that this is usually unconscious. In this scenario, as the team begin to form a series of unspoken decisions about you, *No Invitation* may be the trick they use to limit your ability to make things happen against the interests of the group. The extent to which this happens consciously or unconsciously is fascinating to consider. With other Dirty Tricks in this book, the persecutor is usually operating in the full conscious knowledge of what they are doing; however, this Dirty Trick has an element of 'group think' about it, whereby no conscious, collective decision is made to exclude someone deliberately, and the victim's absence might only be noticed by the group late into discussion.

In our story, we see that Jerry has not invited Surrinder to the day at The Belfry. As old 'sparring partners' or rather 'mortal enemies' Jerry clearly thought it would be to his disadvantage if Surrinder had such ready access to all the key players. He is at a critical point in the Genesis developments and after the SAD he clearly wants to have maximum room to manoeuvre and Surrinder needed to be kept out of the way.

A variation on this trick is when the motive is merely to upset someone. To make them feel ignored, neglected or just feel bad. Irrespective of the motive, if you are a victim of this trick you will probably feel bad. You will start to wonder why it is happening to you.

GAME STATS: NO INVITATION

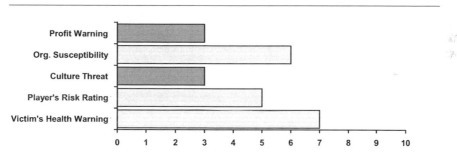

PROFIT WARNING 3/10 (OVERALL, WHAT RISK DOES THIS PRESENT TO THE BOTTOM LINE FOR THE ORGANIZATION?)
Much depends on the issue where the uninvited has a part to play in ensuring that the right decisions are taken. Often when serious issues are being debated, the senior people will notice the absentee and take corrective action.

ORG. SUSCEPTIBILITY 6/10 (HOW PRONE IS AN ORGANIZATION TO THIS TYPE OF BEHAVIOUR?)
With increasing individual competition for airtime, resources and presence the tempta-

tion of using this trick is rising. We have also noticed that the greater the degree of change being pushed through the organization, the more likely this trick will be in play.

CULTURE THREAT 3/10 (HOW DOES THIS AFFECT THE ORGANIZATION CULTURE, AND STAFF MORALE?)
Not a massive threat. This is one of those games that generally gets lost in the busy cut and thrust of working life.

PLAYER'S RISK RATING 5/10 (HOW RISKY IS IT FOR THE PLAYER TO PLAY THIS DIRTY TRICK AND RISK EXPOSURE?)
If you get exposed, you can easily blame it on human error. It is also likely that you'll be able to blame it on someone else's human error! However if you are a repeat offender you are raising the risk that action will be taken against you. Escalation is highly likely if the others you are playing with have rumbled your tactic.

VICTIM'S HEALTH WARNING 7/10 (WHAT RISK IS THE VICTIM PLACED UNDER WHEN THIS TRICK IS IN PLAY?)
At the end of the day, you have been missed off for a reason. With this particular trick it is likely that this reason will put you at a disadvantage in some way. The nature of the risk is dependent on your position within the organization and the issues that you are dealing with.

THE ANTIDOTE: NO INVITATION

The challenging aspect of this game is how easy it is for the gamey individual to claim that it was all just an innocent mistake.

> 'I'm really sorry I left you off the distribution list Jerry, I'll see to it that it doesn't happen again.'

If this is the first time it has happened then it may well be an innocent mistake. It is likely to be a game if the same thing happens more than once, or especially if it is part of a repetitive pattern. You might like to start by asking yourself these self-coaching questions to further your understanding of what is, and what might be going on ...

- What are the facts of this situation?
- How many other examples can I confidently list?
- What am I assuming, imagining or fantasizing about this situation?
- What (innocent) mitigating circumstances might be causing this to happen?
- What might be motivating this individual to miss me off the list?
- Who else might have a covert agenda, and be influencing them to deliberately miss me off the distribution list?
- How do I know this? Is this a fact or a paranoid assumption?
- What are my real feelings about this situation? And, how can I manage these effectively when I intervene?
- What do I not know about this situation? How could I find out?

If, after all this self-coaching, you are convinced that the trick of *No Invitation* is in play, you might like to behave positively and proactively by gently challenging the gamey person. Before you do, think through your approach. The following questions may help:

- What might be the costs or benefits of just ignoring this situation?
- When would be the best time to intervene and challenge so as to get a positive outcome?
- What response might I get from my strategy for intervention?
- What games or excuses might they counter with?
- What will my assertive and professional response be to each excuse?
- What will motivate or encourage them to be honest with me?
- What will motivate or encourage them to respond well when we meet?

Hopefully your answers will start to give you some ideas on what to do next. Unless you have chosen to ignore this trick, you will need to address the individual directly with some carefully selected questions. Your thinking so far will help to equip you to handle the challenge calmly and positively. Remember to choose a time and place for your challenge carefully.

POWER QUESTIONS TO ASK PLAYERS OF NO INVITATION
- Why was I not included on this distribution list?
- What caused me to be left off the list again?
- What is the process for organizing the distribution list?
- Who else is involved in this?
- This is not the first time this has happened, so what is the root cause?
- What process improvements can you suggest?
- What do you think is the net impact of me missing this meeting?
- How would this omission reflect badly on you?
- What could you do to ensure this does not happen again?
- What could I do to help make sure that this does not happen again?

These questions clearly signal your intention not to put up with being left out of the loop, that you are not prepared to put up with the current situation and that improvements must be made. The bottom line is that you must act to ensure that you are involved appropriately in the meetings and decisions that are being taken which relate to you and your work. If someone is determined to thwart your efforts, firm and decisive action needs to be taken. When necessary, a more assertive approach may sound something like this:

> 'Claire, this is still happening and we have spoken about it before, I have the right to be on this list and need you to make that happen, so why don't we have an honest and frank discussion about what is getting in the way here and plan a better process together.'

Before you intervene you will need to reflect on the best practice strategy we have provided and decide how best to adapt it to suit your specific requirements. There is never a guaranteed strategy; however, we believe that if you intervene assertively and professionally along the lines we have indicated, then you will have taken a significant step towards getting a successful outcome. Remember, whatever else happens, if you have acted you will have demonstrated your self-confidence and political savvy. From now on they will appreciate that you are not being taken in by this trick and that you will not get caught out again.

THE POWER OF ...

MISTAKES

A fact of organizational life is that mistakes happen, and the bad news is that we are unlikely to navigate the complexity of a successful career without making them. Being honest about our mistakes, letting the people who need to know about them quickly and with appropriate contrition is a courageous path, but signals our strength and wins more respect than cover-ups, spin or blame spirals. Being honest about a mistake allows others in turn to be honest in their disappointment with us, perhaps even to get upset. But, once declared, the relationship then has more time to recover, trust can be more easily repaired (and probably increased) and an opportunity for learning and development can be taken. Owning our own mistakes and owning up to them is disarming to Machiavellian types. It is the last thing they would expect and they are caught by surprise at our courage and directness.

DIRTY TRICK NO. 17

THE CAUCUS

Coercing people behind the scenes before an important meeting, debate or decision.

As with many of our Dirty Tricks in this book, this very easily masquerades as legitimate activity. What sensible high-performer in any organization will not act to make sure that she has got the support she needs? A positive politician will sound out the views of important stakeholders before a critical meeting so as to be able to plan appropriately and facilitate good business decisions. In developing your ability to influence you have to make sure that you have people aligned with your ideas and also to flush out those that could derail you. Because of this we need to be clear when it becomes a Dirty Trick.

The difference with *The Caucus* is that of motive and means. They are just as determined to get their decision through as anyone else with ambition. They recognize that they are up against the odds, perhaps because there are flaws in their idea. Either there are critical errors in their thinking, or the priorities for the good of the business does not bode well for their motion. This is where personal agendas clash with the organizational imperative. And so to move their personal agenda forward, they caucus and coerce other stakeholders to alter the odds in their own favour.

The Caucus works tirelessly behind the scenes to ensure that their personal agenda succeeds, regardless of the needs of the team or organization. Deviously sounding people out, unfairly 'influencing' or 'tapping' people up so that they can get support for their motion. They have to overcome resistance and better business logic. Their action can include calling in favours or bartering mutual support, but mainly focuses on coercion of others into support. In short, *The Caucus* will use whatever other tactic they can to get people on their side. *The Caucus* believes it is appropriate to bully, manipulate and coerce others before an important meeting, so that on the day, things go 'the right way', which is always their way!

The upside to this Dirty Trick is that the reputation of *The Caucus* usually goes before them so we are already forewarned to some extent. When *The Caucus* comes to see you ahead of the important meeting, they want to know more than just where you stand on the issue before the vote. *The Caucus* wants to manipulate you (using any or all of the games in this book) into supporting their position regardless of your better judgement or what is best for the organization. *The Caucus* wants to load the dice before the game begins. The means of persuasion can be very diverse. Often they will be looking for your weak spots, perhaps by reminding you of how they have helped you out before, or how important their support is for your own goals. If they are desperate they could resort to *Exposure* (see Chapter Four) or worse.

Jerry is clearly in his comfort zone with caucusing. It is fairly obvious that he has used the entire day at the golf course to get people aligned with his position. Perhaps that's one reason why he needed Surrinder out of the way (see No Invitation). The conversation overheard by Ben is a typical indication of caucusing in progress. In this instance, Jerry is calling in a favour granted to the other executive some time ago.

GAME STATS: THE CAUCUS

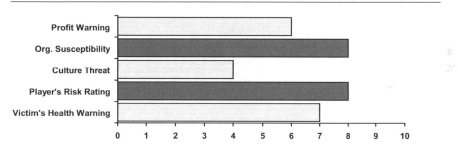

PROFIT WARNING 6/10 (OVERALL, WHAT RISK DOES THIS PRESENT TO THE BOTTOM LINE FOR THE ORGANIZATION?)

If serious caucusing is occurring there must be issues being debated that are serious for the organization. Leaving this unchecked there is a high risk that business critical decisions will be made in favour of self-serving individuals rather than for the benefit of the organization.

ORG. SUSCEPTIBILITY 8/10 (HOW PRONE IS AN ORGANIZATION TO THIS TYPE OF BEHAVIOUR?)

This type of activity is habitual. For the player who is less than honest, the temptation to overstep the mark ahead of big meetings and decisions is frequently irresistible. If the individual stakes are high, the organization will quickly become embroiled caucusing as people endeavour to get into a favourable position.

CULTURE THREAT 4/10 (HOW DOES THIS AFFECT THE ORGANIZATION CULTURE, AND STAFF MORALE?)
This Dirty Trick is just a dent on the culture as people observe others who busy themselves politicking. It raises the political temperature a little but most people see it for what it is.

PLAYER'S RISK RATING 8/10 (HOW RISKY IS IT FOR THE PLAYER TO PLAY THIS DIRTY TRICK AND RISK EXPOSURE?)
This is one of those tricks that people see all too easily. The risk you face is that of becoming labelled as a political animal. This makes people wary in your presence and will be careful what they reveal to you. This lack of openness can seriously affect your future performance.

VICTIM'S HEALTH WARNING 7/10 (WHAT RISK IS THE VICTIM PLACED UNDER WHEN THIS TRICK IS IN PLAY?)
Here the victim has a twofold risk. When complying with *The Caucus* are you being honest with yourself and the organization? What does this do to your self-image of integrity? On the other hand, to deny *The Caucus* your support could open you up to the risk of retaliation from a particularly gamey individual. Tough choice.

THE ANTIDOTE: THE CAUCUS

Handling *The Caucus* when you are on the receiving end can be surprisingly easy. In fact, you don't even need to be convinced that they are caucusing. Next time someone tackles you seeking support ahead of an important meeting, be ready with some penetrating questions.

POWER QUESTIONS TO ASK THE CAUCUS
- What are the facts of the matter?
- What are you really hoping to get out of this conversation?
- What are you suggesting?
- Why would supporting your idea be good for the business?
- How does your idea compare with the other priorities for the organization?
- What is it you want me to do as a result of this meeting?
- Why talk to me about this now? Why not just raise it in the meeting?
- I am wondering why you feel the need to speak to me about this in private?
- What is the real agenda here?
- How do you feel about going behind Ben's back with this?
- What is the cost to you if I decide otherwise?
- What do you stand to gain yourself?
- What lies behind your implication?
- Sorry, I haven't got time for this right now.

The answers you get from this veritable barrage of questions will soon tell you if they are acting with integrity – or not. If their answers are vague and they start to get edgy, chances are that they are playing this trick. At the very least they will be trying to gain your support for a half-baked plan that doesn't really stack up in the light of your questions. Of course it could be just that they are incompetent, but you'll be the best judge of that!

If you suspect that they are playing *The Caucus* you would be well advised to tackle them directly and assertively. The aim of this is to let them know that you are aware of what they are trying to do and will not tolerate this type of behaviour. Choose your words carefully and tailor them to the situation and the individual you are challenging. For example:

'Jerry, it appears to me that you are unusually keen to have my support on this, and I'm not convinced that we both have the same view of what needs to be decided at the meeting for the good of the organization. Can we put our cards on the table and have the real conversation?'

An intervention like this signals your intent to be clear and honest and not to play the game. It also challenges the other person to be authentic and to level with you. Like all our antidotes, there is no guarantee of success, but this approach will dramatically increase your chances of success. The bottom line is they may persist in playing the game, but you get to emerge with your integrity intact.

Perhaps the most difficult to handle is when *The Caucus* is combined with other games such as *Exposure*. This is an insidious combination that needs careful treatment. If you suspect that this is happening, you would be well advised to retreat and consider your options and try to avoid making a hasty or ill-conceived intervention. Remember, that player probably can't be trusted. If you are serious about doing the right thing for your customers, shareholders and the organization you will need to intervene appropriately and skilfully. You will also need to ensure that you keep your job and don't make a 'career decision'.

Make sure and choose your battles strategically. If you have chosen to act then you have already signalled your intention to do the right thing and we are firmly on your side. Adapt the strategy and questions above to suit the needs of your particular situation.

THE POWER OF ...

BIG PICTURE AND MORAL HIGH GROUND

If you have decided to intervene (because this battle is, in your opinion, really worth it) note that in any conversation where a Dirty Trick is present, the more that we enquire about the big picture and what is right for the business the more we indirectly challenge inappropriate politics. It is harder for the politics of self-interest to triumph in the face of politically savvy people, who are determined to do the right thing for the business. The moral high ground and the big picture are often the best arenas for any political battles that need to be fought.

Actively putting self-interest to one side and enquiring about the big picture temporarily depersonalizes the fight and puts the enquirer in a stronger position. Anyone still determined to move forward with a Dirty Trick in the face of such enquiry will have clearly aligned themselves, not with the vision, values and mission, but will be isolated in pursuing their own agenda. Having made our polite enquiries about the bigger picture and taken the moral high ground, we take a sound step towards isolating Machiavelli.

DIRTY TRICK NO. 18

ROCK AND A HARD PLACE

Manipulating people by offering limited or fixed choices expecting the victim to choose the lesser of two evils.

At the heart of this Dirty Trick is the weak or ill-prepared manager who has decided to short-cut authentic decision-making and feels that it is okay to coerce people into doing things that they would rather not do. Having realized that their intended victim will not want to comply, they create a more unappealing or appalling alternative and use this to get the victim to choose to accept the slightly less 'unattractive' option.

Good managers seek to involve those they manage in decisions that affect them. They help their charges to weigh up the pros and cons and come to the right decision. At times we all have to do unpleasant tasks, things that we would sooner not do because they are difficult or potentially damaging to our careers or profile. When faced with this prospect, a great manager will be honest and help us with strategy and tactics and even help us to get used to the idea. They will also work hard to help minimize the risks or unpleasantness.

Some people, however, either don't have time for these niceties or seek to unfairly influence decision-making. Rather than be authentic, they will present an unappetizing choice, usually in the knowledge that when faced with such a choice, you will automatically take the least unpleasant. They offer you Luton or Cumbernauld and sometimes conveniently forget to mention that Florida is also an option! They are not interested in you or your future, just your compliance. By forcing you into the lesser of two evils they save time, and influence you in a way in which – had they been straight with you – you probably would not have chosen. What they have missed is the longer term damage that this does to your motivation and the working relationship between you.

A variation of this Dirty Trick is where someone is offered a difficult 'choice' between two options, but is not alerted to other options. In this version the victim is focused on making a choice between two courses of action, which typically each have a big pay-off for the perpetrator.

At the end of Chapter Six we see the *Rock and a Hard Place* played by Jerry on Ben. To any sane and reasonable person, taking responsibility for the London actions of Genesis, whilst unpalatable, is very much the lesser of two evils! Jerry is relying on Ben's rejection of the Scottish alternative but clearly cannot stop his habit of dressing things up. Lewis also leaves his bystander role to add a final touch to Ben's choice.

GAME STATS: ROCK AND A HARD PLACE

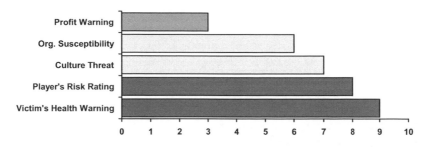

PROFIT WARNING 3/10 (OVERALL, WHAT RISK DOES THIS PRESENT TO THE BOTTOM LINE FOR THE ORGANIZATION?)
Difficult and unpleasant work needs to be done for the good of the organization. In the short-term this can have a positive effect on productivity. However, over time, morale and profitability are undermined by reliance as this tactic of negative motivation progressively affects the bottom line.

ORG. SUSCEPTIBILITY 6/10 (HOW PRONE IS AN ORGANIZATION TO THIS TYPE OF BEHAVIOUR?)
As with many other Dirty Tricks, this is brought on by increasing complexity and pressure brought to bear on busy managers. Rather than learn new ways of motivating their staff it is all too easy for them to fall into playing this trick.

CULTURE THREAT 7/10 (HOW DOES THIS AFFECT THE ORGANIZATION CULTURE, AND STAFF MORALE?)
In essence this is a vicious manipulative tactic that can quickly erode the cultural health of an organization. It is also symptomatic of a more widely practised art of coercive behaviour that can build up into a very negative climate throughout the business.

PLAYER'S RISK RATING 8/10 (HOW RISKY IS IT FOR THE PLAYER TO PLAY THIS DIRTY TRICK AND RISK EXPOSURE?)
You will get exposed. Sooner of later they will work out that you favour this trick. If you want continued high performance from your team over a long period of time you will fail. What will this cost you? Apart from the performance risk, you will also be seen as a manipulative character and reputations like that can spread quickly.

VICTIM'S HEALTH WARNING 9/10 (WHAT RISK IS THE VICTIM PLACED UNDER WHEN THIS TRICK IS IN PLAY)
When this trick is played on you, you can be certain that someone wants you to do something that you wouldn't want to do in a million years. Apart from the unpleasant-ness the risk you face depends on the task facing you in this difficult choice. Your risk is likely to be aggravated by other tricks that may be in play and this could seriously affect your health.

THE ANTIDOTE: ROCK AND A HARD PLACE

Before you get moving on this trick you would be well advised to consider what has been said and how it has been delivered. Engaging your mind before engaging your mouth is a maxim that is certainly worth bearing in mind with this one. To unravel this situation, ask yourself a number of questions:

- Specifically what are the options being proposed?
- To what extent was the unappetizing nature of these options acknowledged?
- How much effort was made to win me over?
- What other options could there be?
- Did I feel like I was being manipulated?
- When thinking of the worst option suggested, how genuine is it?
- Was I given an opportunity to ask questions to help me to decide?
- What does my manager stand to gain from each option?

- How strong is his desire for me to do this?
- To what extent were the options loaded with emotive or personal pleas?
- How much do I trust my manager?

If your responses to these questions start to sound alarm bells, the chances are that a trick is in play and *Rock and a Hard Place* is a frontrunner. In which case, your first step must be to get your emotions in check. You are well within your rights to feel anger and frustration. To give yourself the best chances of dealing with this situation you need to accept these emotions and bring them under control. As soon as we 'lose it' then the manager wins the moral high ground and increases their personal power in the situation. You hand them a huge advantage by failing to manage your emotions.

If this is a game and not just a tough management call, then the manager is attempting to manipulate you into making a choice without the full facts being made available. The manager is gambling on you making the choice in ignorance of other options, which are withheld, or not up for consideration. The secret to confronting this game with integrity is to ask smart questions which are designed to increase the number of options up for consideration as well as inviting the manager into more productive dialogue. That way we get to keep our credibility and integrity and overall, regardless of the outcome of this situation, we enhance our own personal power.

Assuming you make the strategic decision to challenge the *Rock and a Hard Place* at some point very soon you need to engage with the player and ask some sound questions. Choose this moment carefully to maximize the opportunity for the manager to be in the right frame of mind.

POWER QUESTIONS TO ASK IN THE MEETING
- Can you explain the rationale behind the two options?
- What other options are available?
- What can you tell me about the other choices?
- Which would you recommend and why?
- What would happen if I chose neither option?
- Luton or Cumbernauld, how did we end up with these two?

- If I take Luton, who will get Cumbernauld? (or vice versa).
- What if I was to choose something else entirely?
- What if we were to spend a little time generating a better plan?
- What if we worked together to get a solution that worked for both you and me?
- What other information do you have to help me decide?
- What do we not know about this situation?
- Who else will have helpful information that I could talk to?
- What are you not telling me about this situation?

We strongly suggest using the smart questions above as a first intervention since these alone are often sufficient to move the situation on productively. However you may decide that it is more appropriate to take the direct approach. This might sound something like this:

> 'Jerry, these choices just don't ring true to me. I want us to have a more open conversation, so how about we put our cards on the table and talk about what is really happening here and how we can help each other.'

This is a tough conversation as it puts at risk the relationship you have with Jerry; however, we have just flagged up very clearly that we are nobody's fool and that we have the courage and integrity to deal with the situation productively and professionally. In addition we end the intervention by proposing a way forward for them, that we still intend to work productively with them provided a more open dialogue can be had.

This version of the antidote invites more productive dialogue because it has an absence of threat. We don't mention '... or else!' or '... wait till the directors hear about this!' We avoid throwing all our toys out of the pram. We give Jerry another chance to be honest and level with us. We give him a significant opportunity to regain a little of his personal integrity. Sadly all the evidence to date suggests he's not too interested in this last point.

ROCK AND A HARD PLACE

Whatever the specifics of the situation you find yourself in, we are confident that if you choose carefully and adapt the appropriate parts of this best practice to meet your requirements, then you will have taken a sure step in the right direction.

THE POWER OF ...

ASSERTIVE MARTIAL ARTS

The assertive martial artist protects their rights and position and at the same time respects the rights and position of their opponent. The Assertive Martial Artist knows that every action has an equal and opposite reaction and they work with the energy of their opponent. They have learned that in the face of oncoming assault, it is sometimes better to step aside than to confront head on. In the world of organizational politics it is important to be more interested in self-defence than attack. The Assertive Martial Artist does not respond to the threats and invitations from Machiavelli to get manipulative and engage in Dirty Tricks. Just as the martial artist defends rather than attacks, so must you. As you develop your political intelligence remember that the strength and force of Machiavelli is very real, but with skill and dexterity he can be safely disarmed.

CHAPTER SEVEN

DECISION TIME

Jerry's BMW 7 Series swept down the ramp towards the automatic gates of the Xennic underground car park. In the passenger seat sat Lewis, balancing reams of Genesis reports and spreadsheets on his lap. Whilst they waited to be granted entry, Jerry pressured Lewis some more.

'So you are sure that Ben has agreed to your request for help on the outstanding Genesis actions?'

Lewis claimed it was so, that Ben had, much to his surprise, agreed to help, but Jerry was still suspicious. Surely even Ben had worked out what the final death throes of Genesis would involve.

'Right,' Jerry continued, 'this is how were going to play it strategically with the board today.'

Lewis was politely attentive, but inside he was anxious about how it would all go, but at the same time excited to be finally moving in such exalted circles.

'Your role today at the meeting will be to present our rescue plan for Genesis, make the Luton contingent look like they couldn't find their own backsides, using both hands in a brightly lit room, with a map; and save our collective reputations, simple!'

Lewis and Jerry had worked hard over the weekend creating this presentation, designed to ward off Surrinder's accusations and Ben's progress and at the same time expel any suggestion of incompetence on their part. Jerry and Lewis had their story straight and were ready to go. Lewis was thrilled. 'But remember Lewis, the way this works is that I get to ask you some tough questions, just to make it look good, and you get to shine.'

'But what happens if things get hot from elsewhere?'

'Relax, with Surrinder out of the way and the wholemeal, worthy Ben being so naïve there is really very little to worry about. I may be asking tough questions, but we have rehearsed all the answers. Remember I'll be there and will back you up when I can.'

Lewis must have still appeared distracted, so Jerry attempted what he called motivation. 'Come on Lewis, boardroom at 10.30, and next stop Florida.'

Stepping out of the elevator and emerging onto the office floor, Jerry and Lewis went their separate ways to prepare the final touches. Lewis went off to his reserved space in the cube farm, and Jerry to the plush domain that was his office.

'Morning Ann,' Jerry winked at his lovely assistant as he passed her desk.

'Oh Jerry, I am glad I've caught you.' Ann looked concerned. 'The MD is in your office. He's been there since before I got in shortly after eight. Just wanted to let you know.'

Had Ben and Surrinder been witness to this exchange they might have reserved a small smile at seeing the ogre look a little puzzled for once.

'Thanks Ann.' And Jerry headed off to his unscheduled meeting.

The MD was sitting in Jerry's seat surrounded by paperwork. Jerry decided to bluster it out under the old pals act as his first strategy.

'JB, great to see you, enjoy the golf? Put us in the shade again with your handicap.'

The MD frowned. 'Jerry, you may recall I didn't finish the round.' Jerry smiled and looked away. In that moment he looked like a kid who had been caught attempting too much flattery in order to win the approval of his teacher. JB smiled.

'It would still be appropriate for you to shut the door, Jerry.'

'But I have this open door policy I am trying, to make me more approachable. It is based on the feedback.'

Jerry wanted to take this minor opportunity to impress JB by showing him that this was his way of attending to feedback from the 360 process they had run recently. Frankly Jerry thought that 360 feedback was a waste of time; he was not going to change because of some do-gooder in HR and their feedback process.

'Good Jerry, but I still think it would be better if you closed the door.'

Jerry shut the door and sat down in the chair he usually entertained his visitors in. He noticed for the first time how much lower and smaller it was than his own leather-backed, fully automated recliner. JB continued.

'Firstly, do you know why Surrinder was absent from the golf day?'

Jerry fumbled only slightly. 'It was a cock up. Somewhere along the line Ann, Surrinder, Lewis and I got our wires all crossed. Come on JB, everyone knows that Surrinder doesn't know a golf club from a club sandwich.' Jerry noticed that JB was not looking amused, or at his most empathic. Jerry tried a little contrition.

'The bottom line was that she got missed off the list, it was a misunderstanding.'

JB sat forward in Jerry's chair. 'I hope that a misunderstanding is all it was. Surrinder is bringing a claim of harassment against the firm Jerry, and you are specifically named in it.'

Jerry was rocked. 'Harassment, because she was not invited to a damn golf day. You're kidding?'

One look at JB let Jerry know that he was not.

'She lists many specific incidents other than that, so is there anything that you feel I ought to know?'

Jerry was genuinely surprised; he fumbled again and spluttered out something about taking legal advice. JB reassured him that the business was currently running its own internal investigation and that Jerry need not call his lawyer just yet. JB took the conversation off on a different tack.

'I had an interesting chat with Sir Bill last night. He seems to think that there is a bit of a blame battle over Genesis between Luton and London. What's your view, Jerry?'

Jerry was on guard. He had hoped that Lewis would be the front man at the board meeting later and deal with this one.

'Genesis has been fraught with problems from the outset, JB.'

'I'm listening.'

'I was obstructed at every turn with Genesis. Handing over so much control to Luton meant that I was always steering with one hand behind my back.'

'So you're blaming Luton for dropping the ball?'

'Yes, and I am sure that Surrinder will say much the same about London. I'm not blaming the Luton crowd, it's just that I have been powerless to intervene most of the time.'

'Surrinder suggested that I ask you about the list of outstanding actions for London from the last SAD.'

'I've sorted that. Lewis is going to provide an update on all this later today.'

JB looked concerned. Jerry wanted to push an advantage and remind JB that he had even seconded Ben over to Luton to help out, but he kept his mouth shut for a change, still unsure of where this conversation was heading.

'Jerry, my immediate concern today is about the board meeting. If Sir Bill suspects that you and Surrinder are spending more time playing politics than pulling Genesis out of the fire, then it will be trouble all round.'

Jerry was now getting anxious. Being a political fox he somehow sensed that all would not be well at the meeting for him and Lewis, and that other, unseen forces, had been working in the shadows against him. He needed to ensure he was not ambushed at the meeting by the unexpected. Delay was imperative.

'I agree JB, so I strongly advise that we take Genesis off the agenda today and convene a special project task force to review it offline.'

'No Jerry, the old man rightly thinks we have wasted enough on Genesis, it is crunch time for everyone.'

'But if we could just delay for a short while to make sure that we are all on side...'

'Sorry Jerry, Sir Bill has insisted that we go ahead today. I'd like to help but I can't delay again, even if I wanted to.' Jerry noticed his rising panic but did well not to show it. The more JB resisted the more convinced he became that something was up. JB continued.

'And furthermore the agenda is set and everyone is focused and ready to get to work on it. You know that changes to the agenda must be tabled at least a week in advance to ensure everyone can be adequately prepared. No Jerry, we are going ahead as planned.'

'Ben would probably value more planning time, especially as I have asked him to take on more work up in Cumbernauld. A small delay might be in everyone's best interests

... to get the right decision.' Jerry was fumbling again, a last desperate throw of the dice, but one look at JB told him that the MD was not going to be swayed. Jerry acquiesced, and did his best to appear supportive.

'Of course JB, what do you need from me?'

'I need you to toe the company line and give your full support to Ben today. He's got some pretty good ideas about how to proceed with Genesis and I want to get behind him on this one.'

'Alright JB.'

'I have been quietly impressed with Ben. He is tougher than he looks and certainly has the business at heart, which makes a change. I wonder sometimes if I was wrong to let you persuade me to send Mark out to Florida. Okay, see you at the meeting.'

JB left Jerry sitting alone in his office, wondering what the hell he was going to do about the board meeting. He considered for a fleeting moment how things would turn out for Lewis, but it soon passed and he returned his thoughts to ... well ... himself. Eventually he decided to do nothing.

Later, as Jerry headed for the boardroom a nervous looking Lewis intercepted him. 'Jerry, did you know that Sir Bill is here? We didn't plan for that.'

Jerry managed a smile and a reassuring hand on the shoulder. 'Relax Lewis, Sir Bill and I go way back, and remember I am right behind you all the way.'

Jerry pushed back the doors and the two of them strode in with as much bluster as they could muster, and took their seats.

JB in the chair takes no prisoners and kicks straight in demanding the Genesis updates. Genesis is actually item four on the agenda, but JB brings it forward without consultation. The irony is not lost on Jerry who remarks to himself how flexible JB can be about the agenda when it suits him. With a little trepidation, Ben takes the floor and presents his proposal, the one Surrinder resisted so much, and he concentrates on the facts that got them to this position and the immediate damage limitation plan. He is keenly aware that push has finally come to shove! He is careful to avoid casting blame, instead proposing more productive ways forward for everyone. He closes by addressing Sir Bill directly, letting him know that whilst Genesis has had an 'unfortunate' start success is still achievable if his recommendations are fully supported by the board.

Sir Bill looks like thunder but says nothing. JB interjects; thanking Ben for his candour, but before allowing questions turns to Jerry and asks for his input. Jerry signals to Lewis to take the floor.

Lewis picks his way through the creative version of events cooked up with Jerry. He makes some bold commitments, highlights the lack of co-operation 'from some Xennic outstations'; makes some vague promises and then sits down. Difficult questions then emerge from around the table, which Lewis struggles to fight off. He looks to Jerry to support him, but Jerry seems to have taken up a strong interest in his shoes. He avoids his gaze and makes no attempt to stick to the plan. Internally Jerry is scared. A shift in power has occurred and he is in no mood to care about Lewis.

Finally JB turns to Jerry and asks for his personal comments.

'Lewis has worked hard on this presentation on my behalf. I told him what an excellent development opportunity and chance to shine before the board this would be, so I am surprised that his plan should be somewhat vague, and I am disappointed he has overpromised.' Lewis was speechless. He was being hung out to dry. Stunned, Lewis vows to get him, but in a rare moment of common sense decides that now is not the time, and instead he consoles himself with a smooth brushing back of his hair in a last ditch attempt to appear nonchalant.

The rest of the meeting passes by in a dreamlike haze for Jerry. He comes back to the here and now in time to hear JB sum up the meeting and agree to put Ben's rescue plan into action. Furthermore, with a nod from Sir Bill, he gives Ben the resource and time he needs to really turn Genesis around. He takes time to congratulate Ben for his fine work to date and for playing a straight bat. After quickly rushing through the any other business, the meeting closes.

JB intercepts Jerry. 'Can you stay please, Bill and I would like a quick word.'

As the boardroom doors close, Jerry nervously sits down again. It seems that his worst day ever is about to get even worse.

'Jerry, Bill and I have been thinking that a few changes are needed.'

'What sort of changes?' Jerry's internal alarm system is reaching overload.

'Bill and I believe that we need to have a little re-structure, a shake-up. Get some new blood in and move some others on.'

Sir Bill picks up JB's thread. 'Yes, and I am sorry to say that moving Mark out to Florida was not such a great idea after all. Family ties are one thing but this is business. We made a mistake acting on your recommendation, and we intend to recall him.'

Jerry piped up: 'But Mark won't want to come back to London.'

JB and Sir Bill look at each other before turning back to Jerry.

'I suspect that Luton might be a better move for young Mark, given that he still has so much to prove.'

A knock at the door is followed by the appearance of a rather large security guard. JB smiles at Sir Bill as he continues.

'And for you Jerry, this restructure means it is time to attend to your garden.'

In a panic, Jerry is in freefall. 'But I'll sue. Genesis was not all my fault. Look at Lewis, can't you see he is an idiot? And that Patak woman, she's always had it in for me. I'll countersue any move that bloody woman makes.'

Neither JB nor Sir William Henry Smith are to be intimidated however.

'Legal action is of course your prerogative but I am sure that you will find that it will be easier for everyone in these difficult days of change, to co-operate.' Nodding towards the rather huge guard, JB concluded the meeting. 'Dixon has a taxi waiting for you outside. We'll send on your personal effects. Goodbye, Jerry.'

CHAPTER SEVEN: MENTORING INTERVENTION

And so the final political battles are resolved at Xennic. Ben has learned a lot about surviving and thriving in the political battleground, and Jerry finally gets his comeuppance. But what did you make of the way in which the political manoeuvres were played out? Perhaps you thought that everything illustrated here was all above board and just the way that things get done in a large organization. Once again, before we unmask the Dirty Tricks, use the questions below to check your levels of political savvy and raise your awareness.

- What smart moves does Ben make?
- Where does Jerry's plan start to go wrong?
- What should Jerry have done differently in his early meeting with JB?
- What should Lewis have done to protect his own position?
- Why do large projects have such stupid names?
- What could Jerry do to save himself?
- What do you think will happen to Ben in the Epilogue?
- What is the stupid 'in joke' with all the names in the story? If we mentioned that Lewis' first name was John, would you get it then?

All that remains is for us to pick apart the final chapter of the story and describe the moves in these final Dirty Tricks at Work.

THE DIRTY TRICKS IN CHAPTER SEVEN

DIRTY TRICK NO 19: MY HANDS ARE TIED
Pretending to be helpless due to the influence of a higher authority or process, when under the same circumstances but with a different person, there would be a different outcome.

DIRTY TRICK NO 20: WE'RE RIGHT BEHIND YOU!
The tactic of or setting someone up as spokesperson, encouraging risk taking, and falsely suggesting back-up and support, which will usually vanish at the first sign of conflict or problems.

DIRTY TRICK NO 21: RE-STRUCTURE
The tactic of reorganizing a team or department specifically to get an unwanted person out.

DIRTY TRICK NO. 19

MY HANDS ARE TIED

Pretending to be helpless due to the influence of a higher authority or process, when under the same circumstances but with a different person, there would be a different outcome.

The management role will sometimes demand that we enforce policy, rules, processes etc. and make difficult choices and decisions. However, this becomes a Dirty Trick when the rules are enforced for some, but, under the same circumstances, we are more flexible and would bend the rules for another. It is a management bias, a mild form of discrimination, where some employees are rewarded with greater flexibility and apparent understanding from the manager whilst others find that 'rules are rules', and there seems little that can be done to change this.

Management also demands that sometimes it is appropriate to step outside of policies and regulations or to bend the rules in order to get new ideas into our organizations. However, the Machiavellian manager usually uses *My Hands are Tied* as a form of resistance to block ideas which conflict with their personal agenda or to unfairly favour other team members. Clearly this type of negative political activity is worth challenging if it conflicts with the best interests of the organization, its people or its customers. Developing the skills to challenge this appropriately is clearly important if someone you work with is using this tactic to his advantage and to the detriment of the meeting.

The positive intent behind the game is usually one of self-protection, to deflect blame or difficult decisions, tacitly referring the employee to the immovable higher authority, which by implication will not be worth challenging. Even in highly regulated disciplines, as one HR manager put it recently, 'there's always a way.' It can also be used as a mechanism to deflect ideas more easily, which would take lengthy or difficult justifications. Perhaps we just don't have the time today to sit down with Ann and explain all the reasons why her suggestion won't work, so we reach for *My Hands are Tied* and hope that it will be enough to quickly deflect her.

We have also heard examples where this Dirty Trick is combined with the *Creative Magpie* trick we illustrated in Chapter Two, whereby a good idea is blocked using either *My Hands are Tied*, or even *Tell Me More*, and then appropriated by the manager using *Creative Magpie* and passed off as their own work.

The trick of *My Hands are Tied* sends out messages of mild discrimination and favouritism. It highlights management duplicity and damages individual morale because those who find that their ideas are not in favour (or who are not in favour personally) will have to work so much harder and spend more time and energy on the work of influencing legitimate ideas past their gatekeeper bosses. Again this time and energy could be directed into doing beneficial activity.

Notice in our story how Jerry angles to take Genesis off the agenda to protect his own position. Notice also how JB, suddenly switching into the persecutor role, uses this Dirty Trick to cement his entrapment of Jerry into being the victim. Firstly JB suggests that his hands are tied by Sir Bill, then as Jerry fights back, he insists that it would go against the meeting protocol to have an agenda change at such short notice. A little later we have it confirmed that JB is being duplicitous when he freely changes the agenda during the meeting to suit his plans, bringing Genesis from item four to item one, and to keep the heat on Jerry. Also we wonder if, had Ben approached JB with a request before the meeting for delay, whether or not he would have been more flexible? We will never know for sure, but given that Ben's political savvy is increasing, his star is in the ascendancy, he is starting to turn Genesis around and JB has a strong desire to punish Jerry, we think it might have been likely.

GAME STATS: MY HANDS ARE TIED

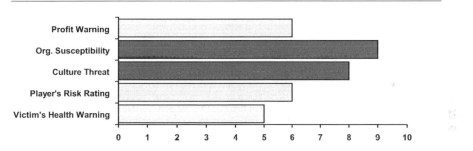

PROFIT WARNING 6/10 (OVERALL, WHAT RISK DOES THIS PRESENT TO THE BOTTOM LINE FOR THE ORGANIZATION?)
The hit on the bottom line will largely be determined by what is being resisted. Where significant performance improvement ideas are blocked by a Machiavellian manager's

political self-interest, then the cost is potentially huge. However we notice from our research that this Dirty Trick is usually about resisting smaller scale ideas or suggestions.

ORG. SUSCEPTIBILITY 9/10 (HOW PRONE IS AN ORGANIZATION TO THIS TYPE OF BEHAVIOUR?)
From the stories that people tell us, this Dirty Trick is extremely common in organizations of all types, particularly in the public sector. Managers view this as a legitimate resistance tactic without appreciating the full impact and likely escalation.

CULTURE THREAT 8/10 (HOW DOES THIS AFFECT THE ORGANIZATION CULTURE, AND STAFF MORALE?)
The impact is greater here than on the Profit Warning scale. This trick undermines the levels of trust in the relationship between employee and manager. It makes the manager appear non-assertive and/or disingenuous and the employee is then strongly tempted into escalating actions.

PLAYER'S RISK RATING 6/10 (HOW RISKY IS IT FOR THE PLAYER TO PLAY THIS DIRTY TRICK AND RISK EXPOSURE?)
Employees are seldom fooled by this trick, despite its proliferation. Politically savvy employees whose antennae have detected this trick in progress and who are assertive enough to want to pressure test the manager are in a potentially strong position and the Machiavellian manager's credibility hangs in the balance.

VICTIM'S HEALTH WARNING 5/10 (WHAT RISK IS THE VICTIM PLACED UNDER WHEN THIS TRICK IS IN PLAY?)
Given that this trick is usually about resisting ideas and requests, the impact is most likely to be moderate on the victim, unless the request is of significant personal importance.

THE ANTIDOTE: MY HANDS ARE TIED

The manager who plays this trick is taking a gamble. They are gambling on you simply accepting the decision of the higher authority or rules and that you won't notice, or know about, the 'special concessions' that they make to other more favoured employees. This means that if you confront them about their duplicity, they are very likely to feel awkward and uncomfortable. If it is merely your intention to 'punish' the manager, then you need not read any further. Just go in there and tough it out or shout at them! However, if you are interested in keeping your dignity and integrity, and increasing your chances of getting what you want, then read on.

The antidote to this game contains several important elements, the first of which is ensuring that we avoid taking an aggressive or adversarial position. It is vital that we do this so as to ensure that we maintain emotional control during the meeting. This increases our personal power and invites the manager into more productive dialogue, and reduces the chance of them starting another game. It is the way we maintain our dignity and integrity. A stand-up fight will only weaken our chances of success and gives the manager more reasons to dismiss the appeal.

Before you meet with the manager, if you know of 'special concessions' that they have made in the past, go and talk to the people involved and who benefited, and find out what the circumstances were. If there is a policy on the matter, go and study it so that you can check that the manager has the details right and notice if there is a right to appeal against the decision. This ensures that when you ask some of the smart questions listed below; you will have the advantage of knowing the facts. The smart questions are designed for you to ask after your initial request has been denied and you have subsequently discovered the manager's duplicity. They also work at the time when you make your initial request, if you suspect this game is being played.

It is understandable that you could feel angry or aggrieved at the manager's stance and duplicity. However, it is vital that you separate the message from the emotion when you meet with the manager. Spend time composing and rehearsing the message before you meet them. Before action, get feedback from a friend or colleague who you trust. Remember that it is okay to talk about how disappointed, annoyed or frustrated you are by their tactics, but it is not helpful to behave in a disappointed, annoyed or frustrated way!

POWER QUESTIONS TO ASK IN THE MEETING
- What would need to happen for this rule to be flexed slightly?
- Under what circumstances has this rule been modified in the past?
- What did your boss actually say when you asked them about my request?
- What were the circumstances under which this rule was modified for Ben?
- In what ways is my request different from his?
- What would be the cost to you of bending this rule for me?
- What if we could come up with some creative ways of making this okay for you?
- How would you feel if I was to talk to Sir Bill (the higher authority) directly?
- What would need to happen for you to be convinced that flexing the rule this time would be the right thing to do?
- How do you really feel about this situation?
- What is getting in the way of you saying yes?

Notice that whilst these questions are challenging, their style and approach is about inviting a more productive dialogue so that you can find out the basis for their resistance. If we can discover the intent behind the Dirty Trick, then we can more successfully neutralize it. And remember, if you are challenging a policy or a decision from a higher authority, ask about any rights of appeal that you may have.

The final part of our proposed antidote strategy is a tough one and should only be used where you are totally convinced that this Dirty Trick is being used, you are calm and controlled and your other questions and challenges have failed. In other words, Machiavelli is entrenched and convinced they are in the strongest position. The key intervention to make is to expose the Dirty Trick, perhaps in a relatively light-hearted manner. Exposing it might sound something like this ...

'JB, I still don't understand why you are blocking this; however, I am disappointed at the manner in which you are doing it. Suggesting that your hands are tied doesn't sound like you, and this surprises me.'

Remember that the one thing that Machiavellian managers are afraid of is for their tactics to be exposed. Once a Dirty Trick is exposed then its power is dramatically reduced and more productive dialogue is often possible. If we then go on to offer JB a way forward or a way out which helps him to still appear okay, then he is much more likely to co-operate.

If all of the above have still failed to be influential, and you are convinced you have the moral high ground, then, and only then, it might be time to consider escalating the situation by either going over JB's head to a higher authority or by appealing to other parties who will support you. We do however only recommend this as a final intervention strategy as it can lead to further escalation and attrition.

THE POWER OF ...

THE RAT'S WAY OUT

Using this book to be more alert and alive to Machiavellian politics is a great idea and we are confident that you will use this information to navigate unhelpful politics rather than engage in them. However, beware of the way of the rat. A cornered rat will raise itself up on its hind legs and attack you. However, offer a rat a way out and it will nearly always take it. When confronting Machiavelli, always ensure that you have a way out, or a face-saving way forward for them. Remember, Machiavelli is heavily invested in the politics of self-interest and that once exposed, his ego may well choose an aggressive strategy, so be ready to ensure that you have left an escape route for him. This does not mean let him win, rather, give him ways out which do not directly threaten him.

WE'RE RIGHT BEHIND YOU!

The tactic of or setting someone up as spokesperson, encouraging risk taking, and falsely suggesting back-up and support, which will usually vanish at the first sign of conflict or problems.

As children, we learn that in the absence of our own self-confidence and assertiveness, we can get others to take difficult issues or requests to more powerful others on our behalf. This is quite appropriate as we have yet to develop these skills and need our parents or guardians to negotiate challenges that we are not yet equipped to navigate ourselves. We also discover that the same is true of our playground gangs and that we can 'volunteer' someone to act as spokesperson either to negotiate with the school authorities or with other playground gangs.

Where things get interesting is the point where we discover that we can scapegoat or punish an unpopular member of our group by 'volunteering' them to negotiate or take messages, which we know will be unwelcome to the receiver. And as part of our coercive strategy we learn that we can motivate a reluctant victim into action by suggesting that we will support them. However the scapegoat quickly gets to discover the duplicity when at the first sign of resistance, the support vanishes.

In the world of work, we notice that this childish strategy is used either as a non-assertive mechanism, or as a scapegoat tactic. In the face of tyrannical or autocratic leadership it becomes a risk to voice an opinion that is out of step with the established order. Therefore, with formal or informal work groups, spokespeople are sometimes sought to take these unpopular views to the tyrant. Heroes or rescuers in the group volunteer to deliver the messages and we respect them for their courage and their assertion, especially if they act selflessly and non-politically. Each of us knows that sometimes the messengers really do get killed! It is quite appropriate to select someone to represent our views who has the skills necessary and will be influential on our behalf. This is after all the basis of trade unionism and good negotiation.

Whilst all of the above is the social dynamic of groups dealing with issues of power and control, albeit in a fairly non-assertive manner, this is nevertheless just the political infrastructure of the organization at work, and this is not so malevolent or unusual. Where this type of activity becomes a Dirty Trick is when it is used as a strategy for political one-upmanship, to punish or scapegoat someone. Where it is a trap we set for an adversary or where we perhaps use up an expendable relationship.

The trick works by suggesting to the victim that if they agree to take the issue forward (and we know, but they are less well informed, about the dangers of doing so) that we will support them. However, we also know that if or when the going gets tough, that our support will be withheld or denied them. In our melodrama we notice Jerry using this tactic over Lewis as they finalize their disingenuous plans to influence the board meeting. *'Remember I'll be there and will back you up when I can.'* And again just outside the boardroom; *'Relax Lewis, Sir Bill and I go way back, and remember I am right behind you all the way.'* And we notice how, when push comes to shove, that Jerry's support evaporates.

GAME STATS: WE'RE RIGHT BEHIND YOU!

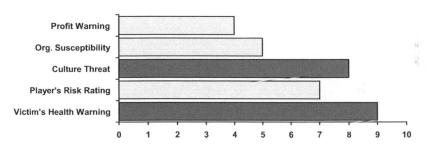

PROFIT WARNING 4/10 (OVERALL, WHAT RISK DOES THIS PRESENT TO THE BOTTOM LINE FOR THE ORGANIZATION?)
As an isolated incident, then not much. But this game usually signals that there is autocratic and unapproachable leadership and that employees are reluctant to be open and honest. This in turn provides the breeding ground for this trick to operate. The longer-term profit warning climbs as ideas are suppressed and more messengers are killed in action.

ORG. SUSCEPTIBILITY 5/10 (HOW PRONE IS AN ORGANIZATION TO THIS TYPE OF BEHAVIOUR?)
The more autocratic or tyrannical the leadership, then the greater the potential for

this game to surface. Where employees enjoy freedom of expression and empathic, but tough management, then the organizational immune system can work as a healthy antidote to discourage this Dirty Trick.

CULTURE THREAT 8/10 (HOW DOES THIS AFFECT THE ORGANIZATION CULTURE, AND STAFF MORALE?)
Given that this is a game of scapegoat it has an initial impact mainly on the victim. Where things get interesting is firstly the malicious time and energy that has been spent by the group in setting the trap, and secondly the escalation and attrition that follow as other stakeholders are invited into the game to rescue the victim, or beat up the persecutors, consuming even more resource.

PLAYER'S RISK RATING 7/10 (HOW RISKY IS IT FOR THE PLAYER TO PLAY THIS DIRTY TRICK AND RISK EXPOSURE?)
The victim of this trick is almost certain to know that they have been set up, so the risk for the game player is in direct proportion to the levels of assertiveness and political power that the victim has. Persecutors should also note that politically savvy victims could use this situation to build alliances with powerful ogres, strengthening their position considerably.

VICTIM'S HEALTH WARNING 9/10 (WHAT RISK IS THE VICTIM PLACED UNDER WHEN THIS TRICK IS IN PLAY?)
If you are set up as the victim of this game it signals a lack of trust and critical weaknesses in your relationships with your team members, and whilst they are unlikely to have the power to fire you, do you really want to work with them in the light of their actions? On the other hand, you are getting more opportunities to develop your survival skills!

THE ANTIDOTE: WE'RE RIGHT BEHIND YOU!

This game is teamwork at its worst. It is the game of getting someone else to take a risk that they wouldn't take without back-up and support, but knowing all the while that there is a different agenda, namely getting them into a difficult position and leaving them alone to struggle. The covert agenda is frequently to get them to make a 'career decision' so that these gamey individuals can benefit from someone else's newly tarnished reputation.

If you have been caught out by this game then you will know how painful it is to be manipulated by colleagues in this way. Your colleagues clearly are a disingenuous and cowardly bunch if this is their idea of teamwork, but you might also like to ask yourself what you did to invite such treatment from them in the first place. Depending on how serious the consequences, they might have just thought that this was a fun way of brightening up a dull afternoon in the office, or right up at the other end of the scale, they might be looking for revenge or to punish you, or to profit in someway from your misfortune. Uncomfortable though it is, the first step in deciding an appropriate strategy is to look inwards and ask yourself what you might have done to invite such an action from them, as well as considering what their motivations might have been.

Clearly you have a right to be disappointed, upset or angry at their behaviour. Use these strong feelings to motivate yourself into taking action, but keep them to one side whilst you actually intervene. It may well be that the pay-off for these gamey individuals is to see you upset, angry or both. They may well be looking forward to seeing you 'lose it' so that they can claim the moral high ground, or perhaps pretend shock or surprise at your behaviour. Turning on them and yelling *'where the hell were you guys?'* is unlikely to get the response you need. Ensure that you do not give them the satisfaction of this small-minded victory.

If you are smart you will know that just letting it go is not a great idea and might encourage them to try harder. A smart strategy is required to stop this from happening again and help you keep your credibility, self-confidence and self-esteem intact. The accepted wisdom emerging from our work is to tackle each person involved in this deception individually. The most potent intervention might sound something like this ...

'Jerry, I am pretty disappointed at your part in what happened. You left me in a very difficult position by not supporting me as agreed. If we are to work well together in the future I suggest that we have a tough conversation about what just happened.'

Of course the really politically savvy individual will not get themself in this game in the first place. If you suspect that you are being set up for this game (or perhaps you are forewarned, having been caught out before) then you might find that some or all of the following smart questions helpful ...

POWER QUESTIONS TO ASK THE PEOPLE WHO ARE 'RIGHT BEHIND YOU!'
• What stops you from taking action yourself?
• Why would you want to support me in taking this forward?
• What makes you think that I would be successful?
• How could I support you in taking this forward for yourself?
• What do you have to gain by getting me to address this for you?
• What specific support are you offering?
• Who else have you asked to take this forward?
• What reasons did they give for declining?
• What happens if I decline your invitation?
• What's in it for me, for taking this risk?

These questions are designed to gently pressure test the position of your colleagues. They are designed to signal the extent of your political savvy and at the same time invite them into withdrawing from playing Dirty Tricks whilst giving you the moral high ground by offering your support in them taking the idea forward.

If you have used some of the questions above and your colleagues are still not invited into behaving with more integrity and credibility, and the situation still does not ring true, then we strongly suggest that you listen to your cautious inner voice. The world of work is becoming a more productive place everyday and there are better teams out there; trust us, we have met and worked with some of them.

THE POWER OF ...

EMOTIONAL INTELLIGENCE

Whatever feelings you are experiencing about this situation can both help and hinder you. Even the allegedly more unhelpful emotions like anger, rage or even wrath can be helpful, if they motivate you into taking positive action. However, it is certainly unhelpful to behave with rage and wrath in any political interaction. Anger is so often responded to by reciprocal anger, thereby fuelling the fire, and a stand-up fight nearly always hands an advantage to Machiavelli who will know how to exploit this. In an argument, the power goes to whoever manages to reclaim their emotional sanity first. It might be appropriate to talk about how angry or disappointed you feel, but always less helpful to be so caught up in your own anger or disappointment that you no longer make any rational sense. It is no longer an appropriate defence to get aggressive and claim later that this is 'just the way I am'. Emotional intelligence can be practised and learned.

DIRTY TRICK NO. 21

RE-STRUCTURE

The tactic of reorganizing a team or department specifically to get an unwanted person out.

As responsible organizations it is appropriate that we 're-engineer' the organization from time to time, usually to align with the mission or vision, and certainly to serve our customers, stakeholders and shareholders better. This usually requires that some people change roles, have responsibilities and reporting structures altered and sometimes these restructures require that some roles are no longer required and that people who are unable or unwilling to change, will need to leave.

However, what is also true is that this can become a Dirty Trick, when the re-structure is really all about jettisoning people, rather than improvement. This game is usually justified as an effective way of getting incompetent or unwelcome people out of our departments or organizations, and it continues to be a popular strategy, because it appears to work.

The downside to this strategy is that when *Re-structure* is used as a Dirty Trick, it is usually recognized as being in play, not just by the management and the intended victim, but also by other bystanders. These bystanders may well be invited to an attempted rescue of the victim, and if these bystanders are powerful or influential then escalation occurs, making the whole process more protracted, painful and more expensive for the organization.

Alternatively the bystanders might be less invested and watch as the organization goes about its strategy. They notice that the real performance management process is not aligned to vision and values and accurate appraisal assessments. They notice instead that the Teflon Law applies. If you are doing good work and keeping in with the powerful stakeholders then almost every transgression will be tolerated. Make a mistake when you are less popular or performance is waning, then *Re-structure* is the unwritten rule.

Re-structure certainly gets rid of unwelcome or unwanted employees, and just as certainly puts another debt on the emotional balance sheet. *Re-structure* clearly signals to the employees the level of duplicity and lack of courage and authenticity of its leadership, and contributes further to the death of the organizational soul.

The financial cost can also be a high one, especially where the game escalates to employment tribunals (complete with resulting bad publicity for the organization if found culpable) or large settlement packages. *Re-structure* is a business as usual process, that promotes constant confusion, rumour and resulting change, during which focus is easily taken away from the market place and customer needs, frequently resulting in competitors gaining an advantage or customers becoming confused and disappointed.

We know of one example where a senior HR manager told us that they (the organization) had never fired anyone in its 43-year history. He also inappropriately likened his organization to South America in the 1980s, at time when citizens just 'disappeared'. Interestingly at the time of this meeting the organization was defending an unfair dismissal case of a senior manager who had recently been restructured and had kept meticulous records of how the organization had conducted itself during other alleged restructures.

The curious aspect to *Re-structure* is its visibility. This game is usually seen from afar by all concerned, even those unconcerned, as it moves inextricably towards its conclusion. As one manager once remarked, 'it was like a car crash in slow motion.'

Bystanders are often unwilling to act in support of anyone being restructured; indeed they are more likely to collude if there is a chance that they might benefit personally from the demise of another's career. Let's be honest, no one is going to be too concerned about bad old Jerry being *Re-structured*, and we will bet that a part of you quietly rejoiced at his downfall (he is our bad guy after all) but the bad news is that our hero Ben, or even you, could just as easily have been the victim. In this case the organization probably came out with the right result, but perhaps failed to calculate the real cost of their process.

GAME STATS: RE-STRUCTURE

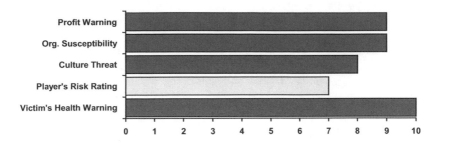

PROFIT WARNING 9/10 (OVERALL, WHAT RISK DOES THIS PRESENT TO THE BOTTOM LINE FOR THE ORGANIZATION?)
The main threat lies in a failure to follow due process, leaving the organization open to legal redress. Not to mention the change management issues, redundancy packages etc. It also has an opportunity cost as energy and attention is wasted managing through the *Re-structure*.

ORG. SUSCEPTIBILITY 9/10 (HOW PRONE IS AN ORGANIZATION TO THIS TYPE OF BEHAVIOUR?)
Used in almost all organizations, as it appears to be a relatively simple and painless way of managing out unwanted individuals.

CULTURE THREAT 8/10 (HOW DOES THIS AFFECT THE ORGANIZATION CULTURE, AND STAFF MORALE?)
Political ostriches apart, everyone usually knows that a restructure is happening and why, despite the often very elaborate strategy documents that are developed to 'justify' the move. The threat to the organizational culture and morale signals the organization's failure to tackle performance issues in line with its own policies and employees cannot fail to notice the duplicity.

PLAYER'S RISK RATING 7/10 (HOW RISKY IS IT FOR THE PLAYER TO PLAY THIS DIRTY TRICK AND RISK EXPOSURE?)

If you are the manager engaging in this game then you are likely to 'win'; however, there is a real chance that something might go wrong with the process and an accusation of unfairness might easily be levelled against you. Ask yourself if playing *Re-structure* really is easier than following the performance management process?

VICTIM'S HEALTH WARNING 10/10 (WHAT RISK IS THE VICTIM PLACED UNDER WHEN THIS TRICK IS IN PLAY?)

If you are being *Re-structured* there is very little that you can do other than to exit with dignity and a suitable full and final settlement. Effectively you have lost the political battle by the time you become aware of your approaching status as a casualty.

THE ANTIDOTE: RE-STRUCTURE

And now we have arrived at our final Dirty Trick for this volume, and we have saved one of the greatest political challenges for last. Surviving a *Re-structure* (when it is a Dirty Trick) is possible, just very difficult; and under most circumstances if you are on the receiving end, then it is very often about exiting with dignity, credibility and a fair settlement. There is usually an internal appeals process, which you might be able to invoke successfully and retain some sort of role within the organization, but it is very unlikely that your role will be unchanged since this would involve a U-turn on the part of the persecutors. It might also be possible to mobilize sufficient political clout to challenge the outcome, but again, by the time you get wind of the fact that you are being *Re-structured*, then it is probably too late.

Once outside of the organization, there are legal rights of redress that might be invoked if you can prove that you have been unfairly treated or discriminated against. However, none of these processes are likely to be able to reinstate you, and even if they were, would you really want to go back? When someone is *Re-structured*, either as part of a valid process or as a victim in a Dirty Trick, the tough bottom line is still the same;

the organization has declared that their time is up, the immune system has kicked in, and they are expected to leave, preferably without too much fuss.

If you suspect that you are being *Re-structured* then the first step is to do all you can to check for evidence that this is a fact, rather than a paranoid fantasy. Paying attention to watercooler gossip is all very well, and this grapevine can be highly accurate, but you need something harder on which to base future actions. Because *Re-structure* is a relatively slow moving game (the organization needs time to check that due process is being followed and that a heavy lawsuit will not be the outcome) then initially, time is on your side. The first part of the strategy for managing yourself safely through a *Re-structure* is to use this time to your advantage, checking out your conspiracy theory with anyone you know who might have information to confirm or refute your gut feeling.

It is obviously worth talking to anyone who you know and trust who might be able to help you; however, under these circumstances it might also be worth talking to your adversaries and opponents as they might well leak clues about what might be going on out of your sight. Engaging directly with adversaries who are likely to either profit from your demise, or perhaps enjoy the sense of victory at your downfall, can be very revealing, especially if they are careless, or unprofessional enough to gloat. Go see them, ask them about their views or even advice (remember you don't have to take it) but pay really close attention to what they say and how they say it. Remembering that 93% of communication is non-verbal, so try listening to the music as closely as the words!

Try asking some or all of the following smart questions of your stakeholders, allies and even adversaries to check more deeply for the real reasons. Any data gathered in these meetings might be highly valuable later and will form the basis of what to do next. We have advised some people to make extensive notes in order to create an audit trail, which might be needed later. These are smart generic questions and depending on your situation and the specific nature and type of organization, some adapting may well be necessary to sharpen them up.

POWER QUESTIONS TO ASK ABOUT THE ALLEGED RE-STRUCTURE

- What do you know about the rumoured restructure?
- What are the main drivers behind this restructure?
- How long will the restructure process take?
- When will there be some sort of official announcement?
- How will we minimize the disruption to the business?
- How will this restructure help us to serve our customers better?
- What process will be used to determine and allocate new roles?
- What specific criteria will be used?
- Who will be involved in the decision-making process?
- Who will have the final say?
- How will the business ensure fair play during the process?
- What right of appeal will there be?
- Who will be affected by this restructure? (ask about people, jobs, how many, how soon?)
- How will I be affected by this restructure?
- How will the results of the restructure be communicated? (And when?)
- How will the restructure be communicated to our customers and suppliers?
- What opportunities are there for using this restructure to perhaps change career or move into a different role?

Remember to be polite and tenacious as you ask, and look closely at speaker who may well be unintentionally 'leaking' clues about how honest they are being. Notice the extent to which responses sound or look defensive. You might like to use this as a cue to a follow-up question such as *'You seem pretty uncomfortable about talking about this, what is on your mind?'* or *'what is really going on?'*

Some people have remarked that asking questions is a risky business and increases your chances of being 'restructured'. The ostrich tactic seems to be many people's preferred approach. We beg to differ. It is certainly an act of courage to engage the powerful people in the organization with these questions; however, remember that if this really is a game of restructure and you are the intended victim, by the time you are told about it and then invited to ask your questions, the decisions have in all probability already been made. Asking tough questions is unlikely to increase the 'career threatening' element for you personally. But asking them might well demonstrate your confidence, personal power and political savvy, and sends out a strong signal.

Optionally, depending on the situation you may wish to escalate the directness of your approach, with care along the lines of:

> 'JB, no one believes that this restructure is anything other than managing me out of the organization. I think that this situation is already uncomfortable enough for everyone, so let's work together and find the best way forward.'

If the powers that be in your organization are deluded enough to think that restructure is a good way of managing unwanted people out, and furthermore that bystanding employees are so dumb that they won't realize that this is a game, then asking about the methodology and reasons behind previous 'restructures' should prove awkward for them, and perhaps helpful for you. It might sound something like this ...

> 'The word around the business is that this process is used to get unwanted people out of the business, so how might you reassure the team that this is not the case?'
>
> 'We restructured just last month and the word is that it was more about getting rid of Fraser. What might you say to reassure people this time round?'

If as a result of your enquiries you get either anecdotal or better still, hard copy evidence, that there is some disingenuous activity happening, then you have a moral dilemma and some difficult choices ahead. Where this is the case then you need independent advice about how best to proceed and maximize your position. The bottom line is that you need to decide what you want from the situation as an outcome. Identifying your best and worst scenarios and discussing these with your professional advisers will be a good next step.

Remember, if the organization really does want you out, do you really want to stay? If you confront the organization with evidence of its own duplicity, do you really believe that they will back down? Yes, sometimes they can be dissuaded, but realize the extent of the challenge you are taking on. Remaining inside the organization under these circumstances probably means limited scope for progression. We are reluctant to suggest this, but you are likely to be much better off exiting with dignity and credibility intact, a good settlement in the bank and a good reference to post before future employees. Be reassured that there are better organizations out there to work with, so put some energy and attention into finding them!

However, before you rush off to make that appointment with the headhunter, take a few minutes for quick reflection. The final uncomfortable truth about being the victim of *Re-structure* is that at some level, you made a mistake which prompted their action, so put the pain aside for a second and be honest about what you might have done to prompt it. We are not suggesting that you deserved it, but this Dirty Trick is usually invited, at least in part, by the victim. Where has your performance been less than it should? Which powerful people might you unwittingly have crossed? What rules or rituals might you have bent or broken? Understanding what the catalyst was will better help you ensure that you are not condemned to make the same mistakes again.

A FINAL MESSAGE TO THE MANAGER WHO THINKS 'RE-STRUCTURE' IS A GOOD STRATEGY

If you are the manager or leader of an organization and you think this is a good way of addressing poor performance or managing 'difficult' people out, then see if you have the courage to ask yourself the same questions we asked earlier. Consider how uncomfortable it might get, if the people you are restructuring have developed an ethical strategy to challenge you. If you are still determined to press ahead, then ask yourself this next set of questions.

- Do you really think that your people will be ignorant of the real agenda?
- What level of trust will exist between you and the employees that remain, after the game is finished?
- How long will it take morale to recover from this strategy?
- Is this really how you want to do business?
- Is this really the sort of organization you want to build?
- Is this strategy really in line with your own personal values?
- What might the personal cost be to you?
- What might all the hidden costs of this strategy be?
- What impact will this strategy have on your customers?
- What might the legal consequences be if you are caught out?
- Can you afford the negative publicity of being exposed as a poor place to work[1]?
- What really stops you from dealing with this situation professionally?
- Whilst the restructure is in process, how effective do you believe your people will be? How motivated, focused and committed will they be? Can you really afford it?
- What might this say about your own values, ethics and moral courage?

If you are starting to reconsider your belief in *Re-structure* as a legitimate tactic for your organization you now have some tough choices ahead. Here at the close of this book, we hand you a dilemma. You clearly have some entrenched habits on how to handle work situations. Are you up for a change? Can you cope with a more authentic approach? If not, as the popularity of this book increases, your exposure risks are rising. The choice is yours.

---

[1] We recently heard someone declare that they would never work for the major employer in their town because 'they are always re-structuring, they must be in trouble.'

RE - STRUCTURE | 229

THE POWER OF ...

SURRENDER

We need to accept that just as we don't need to fight every battle that comes our way, we won't win every battle we fight. Sad but true. Some Machiavellian types are so determined and mired in their own faulty, manipulative thinking that they just won't be invited into behaving authentically and creatively. They have not learned the connection between relationship and results, and are caught up in short-term thinking. In some cases it seems that the more we invite and encourage them to be authentic, the more they play games. There will be times when we have to surrender and let it go, either in the face of overwhelming force or because the issue is just not important enough. There will be times when it is more important that we keep our integrity, self-esteem, careers and values intact and allow Machiavelli a small victory. The quicker we decide to let the small stuff go, the quicker that we can direct our energies and attention to more appropriate challenges.

EPILOGUE: FLORIDA - SIX MONTHS LATER

Hanna took in the wonderful view from their Florida beachfront complex. Down at the water's edge, Ben was enjoying himself splashing and paddling with the kids. It was good to see him relaxed. Hanna couldn't remember the last time Ben had really switched off. And, after the troubles of the last year, he really deserved it.

'My parents were disappointed that I didn't go back home with Mark, but how could I leave all this?' Miranda swept her hand out to indicate the vista of their Florida beachfront complex. 'Another G 'n' T?'

Hanna nodded in reply. 'I can't say I blame you for staying. After all, Luton is, well ... Luton.' When Mark had left, he promised Miranda it would only be for six months or so while he 'proved himself'. Miranda wasn't waiting. If he had failed to meet her father's expectations perhaps he hadn't met hers either? So, she had stayed put in Florida with JB finding something to keep her occupied.

Hanna sat back on the lounger. 'It was really good of your father to let us stay here, and it's nice being able to get to know you at long last.'

Miranda smiled. 'Daddy said that you and Ben should take a little break, particularly given the way Ben dug him out of the proverbial with Genesis. Now it looks like your chap is going to bring the whole thing to a satisfactory conclusion.'

'But not without a few trials along the way!' Hanna smiled. She wondered what on earth had happened to Jerry. Ben told her that most people around Xennic were surprised at just how little difference Jerry's rapid departure had made. Of course he was missed, but only like one misses having a hole in the head.

'So, tell me Hanna, would you like to settle over here?'

'Ooohh, that's a tough call, Miranda.' There was a moment of silence between them before both women laughed at Hanna's sarcasm. Over the last week they had become firm friends and Hanna was very impressed. Not only was Miranda good fun to be around socially, she was clearly making strong progress building up the latest US subsidiary of Xennic.

'Daddy will be pleased you like it here.'

'However, I do need to keep Ben's feet firmly on the ground after what happened last year. Wouldn't do to get too carried away.'

'Yes, but it was funny, especially when Surrinder was given Jerry's job. That said, she did not look very pleased when Daddy broke the news.' After a little pause, Miranda continued, smiling. 'Technically, of course, she just took on some new responsibilities, it was a *re-structure* after all.'

'What's the difference?' Hanna was puzzled. Although she kept up with most things to do with her husband's work, some things still passed her by.

'Something legal I'm told.' Hanna made a mental note to mention this to Ben, yet she was confident that he would know all about it. She was a little concerned in case Ben got caught up in some new Dirty Tricks. Perhaps the games had just moved on to another level in Xennic, or perhaps Americans had their own political games and power plays?

Before she had time to reply, Ben came bouncing up with a big smile on his face, clearly happy with life. Hanna ruffled his hair. 'You look like you're enjoying yourself, Ben?'

'Yes, but I must confess I've not kept my promise?'

'Promise?'

'Yeah, that I'd not think about work. I just saw a crab crawling under a rock and it reminded me of Lewis, made me smile.'

'Oh that creep,' chirped in Miranda.

'What's he up to these days, apart from crawling under rocks?' Hanna asked.

'Well, just before we left to fly here, we heard he's being transferred to a new department. I wonder how Lewis will feel when he learns that training is being relocated to Cumbernauld!'

Miranda laughed so hard that G&T nearly shot out of both nostrils. 'I heard that too, I just hope for all our sakes that his first course is not about building a positive image. If those graduate trainees listen to their new trainer, it could be career limiting.'

With good spirits, all three clinked glasses and toasted Florida.

EPILOGUE: MENTORING INTERVENTION

When we first started Politics at Work, and began writing and researching this book, we easily and quickly identified these Dirty Tricks, along with many more. We then discovered that the managers whom we worked with not only identified with our early catalogues of mischief, they took great delight in telling us their stories, converting these into games with pithy titles and devising countless variations on a theme. We are now in a position to threaten our publisher and long-suffering editor John Moseley with an almost endless series.

We have been fortunate to have worked in some of the largest corporate organizations, and run workshops and seminars for their most talented managers. These experiences nearly always throw up the same themes.

- Most managers (indeed most employees) in organizations want to do good work and ...
- The majority were not impressed when they encountered colleagues who used the type of Dirty Tricks exposed in this book.

- Some brave souls were honest enough to tell us that they did indulge in these tactics and were ambivalent about this; with some of them considering that this is 'just the way things get done around here' or 'that's life'.
- A few were even brave enough to suggest to us that they were ignorant of this type of activity, were uncomfortable about our work, but now recognized that they were usefully forearmed against negative politics.
- Some enlightened managers recognized that these negative political acts were likely to set off an unfortunate chain reaction as other bystanders 'got involved' but most considered the threat from negative political acts very myopically.
- Too few, really, considered the consequences of these acts on the organization in terms of time, money, lost customers and contracts, disillusioned talent leaving, reputation damage, stress, breakdowns, heart attacks etc.
- And, most worrying of all, when the fun with the catalogues and discussion about negative politics was over, we challenged them as to what the antidotes were to such negative bureaucracy. We were mostly met by vacant expressions, much shoulder shrugging and shoe gazing. The other popular alternative to this was using more Machiavellian politics to counteract Machiavellian politics, which only exacerbated the problem.

This apparently paralysing mix of ambivalence and ignorance does not bode well for the political health of our organizations. Indeed, most of the evidence we have collected and experiences we have had suggests the opposite. The distinguished management research organization Roffey Park have researched this subject extensively, and their papers clearly indicate that, unless we take action, the ailing patient that is our organiszational culture, is heading for terminal arrest.

The challenge for leadership is immense, especially given that we all take our cue about how to behave from the top. But where to begin? Here are a few pointers.

1 Open the debate
In many respects this is the hardest part. To raise the possibility that some of our most senior people are not behaving ethically, indeed are behaving with rampant self-inter-

est, is a risk. We have learned that to raise the subject of power and politics in organizations is to stir up profound and uncomfortable feelings and experiences for most of people. But if we are to have strong leadership, then one of the big new challenges is here. We need to get the drag this uncomfortable topic out of the shadows (where Machiavelli does his most potent work) and into the light.

2 Learn and up-skill

Despite the initial paralysis of the managers we have worked with, positive and effective political skills can, and indeed must, be taught more explicitly at every level of the organizational management structure. If managers are learning politics from their peers and seniors, what sort of politics are they learning?[1] Remember that the fish rots from the head! Given the lack of awareness and lack of choices that many managers feel in these situations, good management development programmes need to be devised to provide better influencing skills. Of course, as providers of such services we would say that wouldn't we, but can we all continue to ignore this threat to our organizational survival?

3 Politics is necessary

Recognize that politics is a necessary part of organizational activity and that it is not going to go away, indeed there is strong evidence to show that it is on the increase.[2] Therefore, plan to take action to breed a culture of positive politics.

4 Corporate values

Revisit the corporate values to ensure that these align with positive political behaviours. And, before you say 'hey, we're okay, we've got "act with integrity" on a nice laminate card,' ask yourself: what does that look like, sound like or even feel like? How will we

---

[1] '42% of people learned political skills from others, 27% learned instinctively, 24% through bitter experience and 7% have not learned.' Source: Roffey Park.

[2] '69% of respondents in the 2002 survey reported that political behaviour was rife – and on the increase.' Source: Roffey Park.

know integrity when we encounter it? How explicitly have you described the type of political activities that are acceptable and those that are not? Also, consider if your reward and motivation structures support such values. If not, change them!

5 Don't underestimate Machiavelli

Remember that fighting Machiavellian politics is a massive organizational performance initiative waiting to happen. Imagine if you no longer had to 'play games' to get things done? How much more rewarding would your work become? How much more effective could you and the team become? Imagine the step change in the performance of your organization. Dare to imagine that a more positive political organisation is possible.

And as for you as an individual? Where do you start building your political skills, especially if the rest of the organization is just not ready to get enlightened yet? Waiting for the organization to change to a more positive political culture is probably to wait in vain. We suggest that, given more and more people are approaching us about learning positive politics, those who add power and politics to their personal development plan now will gain an advantage when it comes to advanced level influencing skills. Not only will they be ahead of the game, they will also be better able to act with integrity, build longer term credibility and be true to their personal values.

A personal starter for ten includes …

1 Positive attitude

Get a positive attitude to organizational politics. It is not going away, it is getting more complex by the day, so get your head out of the sand and get learning. Where possible get some professional development in this area. Talk to HR or the training department about the possibility of adding this fascinating and vital subject to the organization's development timetable and strategy.

2 Involve others

Discuss this book and the Dirty Tricks with other friendly and enlightened souls you can trust. Discuss the type of unhelpful politics you encounter and use the ideas in this book to work for you in beginning to building up your own and the organization's immune system. Buy lots of copies of this book and share them around everyone you work with.[3]

3 Discard books
Throw away any books about power and politics that advocate destructive, one-up, Machiavellian, manipulative politics. These flat earth thinkers have had their day.

4 Suspend emotion
When you encounter Dirty Tricks (and now you'll know it when you see it) then suspend your emotions and get intelligent, remember to ask better questions and keep calm.

5 Moral high ground
Look for the moral high ground and the bigger picture whenever you encounter myopic self-interest. This is always a tough place for Machiavelli to hide.

6 Help Machiavelli
Always have a 'way out' or 'way forward' to offer Machiavelli. Remember that a cornered rat will attack, but if you give it an escape route, it will always take it.

7 Influence with integrity
Use your personal power ethically and appropriately. We have shown time and again that there are better ways of dealing with negative politicking without joining the fray. We strongly encourage you to take heart and give it a go.

---

[3] Editor's shameless footnote!

And here our first book ends. We hope that you have been entertained as well as challenged and enlightened. In addition, we very much hope to recruit you to the crusade against negative politicking and abuses of power in organizations. Remember that we have the moral high ground and the best interests of the organization at heart and that this is also mutually inclusive of us succeeding as individuals too. Together we can get Machiavelli on the run and give him no place to hide.

Mike Phipps and Colin Gautrey
March 2005

APPENDIX ONE:
BIBLIOGRAPHY

Over the last few years we have worked and studied hard as we built our understanding of the world or power, influence and organizational politics. Here are a collection of just some of the books and papers we found particularly interesting.

Adams, Scott. (1992) *Build a Better Life by Stealing Office Supplies,* Nicholas Brealey.

Anuinis, Herman and Henle, Christine. (2001) Effects of Nonverbal Behavior on Perceptions of a Female Employee's Power Bases, *Journal of Social Psychology,* **141;4**.

Argyle, Michael. (1967) *The Psychology of Interpersonal Behaviour*, Pelican.

Aristotle. (1991) *The Art of Rhetoric*, Penguin.

Back, Ken and Back, Kate. (1982) *Assertiveness at Work*, McGraw-Hill.

Bell, Derrick. (2002) *Ethical Ambition*, Bloomsbury.

Berne, Eric. (1964) *Games People Play: The Psychology of Human Relationships*, Penguin Books.

Block, Peter. (1993) *Stewardship: Choosing Service over Self-Interest*, Berrett-Koehler.

Block, Peter. (1987) *The Empowered Manager: Positive Political Skills at Work*, Jossey Bass.

Brandon, Rick and Seldman, Marty. (2004) *Survival of the Savvy*, Free Press.

Brown, J.A.C. (1963) *Techniques of Persuasion*, Pelican.

Carlson, John R. *et al.* (2000) The Relationship Between Individual Power Moves and Group Agreement Type, *Advanced Management Journal* **65;4**.

Carnegie, Dale. (1959) How to Win Friends and Influence People, various publishers.

Ciampa, Dan. (2005) Almost Ready: How Leaders Move Up, *Harvard Business Review* **83; 1**.

Clarke, Jane. (1999) *Office Politics : A survival guide*, The Industrial Society.

Cohen, Allan R. and Bradford, David L. (2005) *Influence Without Authority*, John Wiley & Sons Inc.

Corbett, J. Martin. (1994) *Critical Cases in Organisational Behaviour*, MacMillan.

Covey, Stephen R. (2004) *The 7 Habits of Highly Effective People: Powerful Lessons in Personal Change*, Free Press.

Darr, Wendy and Johns, Gary. Political Decision-Making Climates, *Human Relations* **57;2**.

Deluca, Joel R. (1999) *Political Savvy; Systematic Approaches to Leadership Behind the Scenes*, EBG Publications.

Dobson, Michael S. and Dobson, Deborah S. (2001) *Enlightened Office Politics*, Amacom.

DuBrin, Andrew. (1990) *Winning Office Politics*, Prentice Hall.

Egan, Gerard. (1994) *Working the Shadow Side: A Guide to Positive Behind-the-Scenes Management*, Jossey Bass Wiley.

Eran, Vigoda-Gadot *et al.* Politics and Image in the Organizational Landscape, *Journal of Managerial Psychology* **18;8**.

Gallwey, Timothy W. (2000) *The Inner Game of Work*, Villard Books.

Goleman, Daniel. (1996) *Emotional Intelligence*, Bloomsbury.

Greene, Robert and Ellfers, Joost. (2000) *The 48 Laws of Power*, Profile Books.

Handy, Charles. (1995) *The Age of Unreason*, Arrow Books.

Handy, Charles. (1976) *Understanding Organizations*, Penguin.

Harris, Thomas A. (1970) *I'm Okay, You're Okay*, Pan Books.

Hawley, Casey. (2001) *100+ Tactics for Office Politics*, Barron's.

Hay, Julie. (1993) *Working it out at Work: Understanding Attitudes and Building Relationships*, Sherwood House Publications.

Ing-Chung, Huang *et al.* (2003) The Role of Burnout in the Relationship Between Perceptions of Organizational Politics and Turnover Intentions, *Public Personnel Management* **32;4**.

Kennedy, Gavin. (1982) *Everything is Negotiable*, Random House.

Kennedy, Gavin. (2000) *Influencing for Results*, Random House.

Kiesler, Charles A. *et al.* (1969) *Attitude Change: A critical Analysis of Theoretical Approaches*, John Wiley & Sons.

Koch, Christian. (2000) The Ventriloquist's Dummy? The Role of Technology in Political Processes, *Technology Analysis & Strategic Management* **12;1**.

Kuzmits, Frank *et al.* Using Information and E-mail for Political Gain, *Information Management Journal* **36;5**.

Lausch, Erwin. (1975) *Manipulation: Is your brain your own?* Fontana.

Longenecker, Clinton O. and Gioia, Dennis A. (2000) Confronting the Politics in Performance Appraisal, *Business Forum* **25;3/4**.

Lyle, Sussman *et al.* Organizational Politics: Tactics, Channels and Hierarchical Roles, *Journal of Business Ethics* **40;4**.

Machiavelli, Niccolo. (1970) The Discourses, Pelican.

Machiavelli, Niccolo. (c.1640) *The Prince*, various publishers.

McAlpine, Alistair. *The Servant: A New Machiavelli*, Faber and Faber.

Michaelson, Gerald Á. (2001) *Sun Tzu: The Art of War for Managers*, Adams Media.

O'Brien, Paddy. (1992) *Positive Management – Assertiveness for Managers*, Nicholas Brealey.

O'Connor, Wendy E. and Morrison, Todd G. (2001) A comparison of Situational and Dispositional Predictors of Perceptions of Organizational Politics, *Journal of Psychology* **135;3**.

Pan, Gary and Flynn, Donal. (2003) Information Systems Project Abandonment: A Case of Political Influence by the Stakeholders, *Technology Analysis & Strategic Management* 15;4.

Peck, M. Scott. (1988) *People of the Lie: The hope for healing human evil*, Arrow.

Pfeffer, Jeffrey. (1994) *Managing With Power: Politics and Influence in Organizations*, Harvard Business School Press.

Quick, Thomas L. (1985) *Power Plays: The Key to Performance and Success in Business*, Cedar Books.

Richards, I.A. (1936) *The Philosophy of Rhetoric*, Oxford University Press.

Rozakis, Laurie and Rozakis, Rob. (1998) *The Complete Idiot's Guide to Office Politics*, Simon & Schuster.

Salmon, William. (1998) *Office Politics for the Utterly Confused*, Schaum.

Schrijvers, Joep P.M. (2004) *The Way of the Rat*, Cyan Books.

Stewart, Ian, and Joines, Vann. (1987) *TA Today : A New Introduction to Transactional Analysis*, Lifespace Publishing.

Tannen, Deborah. (1994) *Talking from 9 to 5: Women and Men at work, Language, Sex and Power*, Virago.

Valle, Matthew and Witt, L.A. (2001) The Moderating Effect of Teamwork Perceptions on the Organizational Politics-Job Satisfaction Relationship, *Journal of Social Psychology* **141;3**.

Valle, Matthew *et al.* (2002) Dispositions and Organizational Politics Perceptions, *Journal of Management Research* **2;3**.

Vigoda, Eran. (2000) Internal Politics in Public Administration Systems, *Public Personnel Management* **29;2**.

Whitney, John and Packer, Tina. (2000) *Power Plays: Shakespeare's Lessons in Leadership and Management*, MacMillan.

Wijnberg, Nachoem M. (2000) Normative Stakeholder Theory and Aristotle: The Link Between Ethics and Politics, *Journal of Business Ethics* **25;4**.

Witt, L.A. *et al*. (2000) The Role of Participation in Decision-Making in the Organizational Politics-Job Satisfaction Relationship, *Human Relations* **53;3**.

Zanzi, Alberto and O'Neill, Regina M. (2001) Sanctioned versus Non-Sanctioned Political Tactics, *Journal of Managerial* **13;2**.

APPENDIX TWO: ABOUT POLITICS AT WORK LTD

Politics at Work Ltd specializes in helping individuals and teams develop their capability to influence with integrity. Organizational life can get very political, stressful and unpleasant at times, so Politics at Work exists to enable our clients to cut through time-wasting and de-motivating negativity, by developing positive political skills.

With the cost of unhelpful politicking now being measured in billions, the development of political skills can no longer be left to chance. Politics at Work provides organizations with renewed hope for better results through original ideas and tried and tested development interventions, focused exclusively on power, influence and organizational politics.

www.politicsatwork.com

ABOUT THE AUTHORS

MIKE PHIPPS

Mike is fast becoming one of the UK's leading authorities on Organizational Politics and Positive Personal Power. As a consultant and trainer, he has worked with over 30 of the world's largest and most prestigious organizations. This extensive experience has built within him the capability to relate quickly and easily to managers and directors in tough, fast-moving, political environments. His style is outgoing, personable and approachable, with an ability to cut through the political nonsense, and achieve more productive outcomes.

COLIN GAUTREY

As a professional businessman, mentor and coach, Colin has a real appreciation for the complexities of the modern business world and, inevitably, this experience has been gained in some highly political environments. This breadth and depth of experience is combined with a penetrating intellect, an intuitive grasp of priorities and a relentless, determined attitude; all of which contribute to the impressive results our clients achieve. His formidable track-record could only have been achieved with a keen ability to influence on all fronts.

INDEX

Printed and bound in the UK by
CPI Antony Rowe, Eastbourne